9
Chances
to
Feel Good
About
Yourself

Judy A. Laslie

Judy A. Laslie

Original art and design on cover by Judy A. Laslie

Typography by Pacific Vision

Library of Congress Cataloging-in-Publication Date
Laslie, Judith A.
9 chances to Feel Good About Yourself
Laslie, Judith A.

First Edition
Second Printing 1997
1. Non-fiction, holistic approach to loving your life in self-help form
TXU 318 437
ISBN 0-9650218-3-1

Dedicated to Beverly Joan Berning (1935-1954)
I never said good-bye

I said a Prayer for you today
    And know God must have heard
I felt the answer in my heart
    Although He spoke no word.
I didn't ask for wealth, or fame
    (I knew you wouldn't mind).
I asked Him to send treasures
    Of a far more lasting kind.
I asked that he'd be near you
    At the start of each new day
To grant you health and blessings
    And friends to share your way.
I asked for happiness for you
    In all things great and small.
But it was for His Loving care
    I prayed the most of all.

Grateful acknowledgment of the contributions by
Rosemary DeLancey, Elizabeth Demaree, John Davis,
Mary Quackenbush, Ruthann Walsh and Ralph Venturi,
Clara Magill, Marilyn Lyman,
Rosemary Squires and Carolyn Hall, Dave Biggs,
Barbara Turner, Dick Rappleye, Russell Jalbert, Connor Mills,
Betty Bielat, Dennis Fairchild, Hazel Dawkins and Kyo Takahashi
toward making the good news in this book possible.

Also, loving thanks and appreciation to
very special parents who encourage me to grow;
my college sweetheart husband and best friend who inspires
and supports my growth;
and our three wonderful adult children who also help me grow.

You are *all* my teachers.

We may never know where our influence leads,
Or if favor is found in all of our deeds.

Excerpt from "God's Flowers"
B. H. Wann

Contents

Preface   ix

Accept You — Choices — Perceive, Believe, Feel — Proof — What
You Want — "The Woman at the Well" — What You Can Expect.

Part I
Explanation of Life

Ours   1

Our Energy Source — Our God Nature — Our Reality — Our Brain
Receiver — Prayer — Problems — Opportunities — Live in the
Present — Cop-outs — More Cop-outs — Life with Our Body —
Thoughts Manifest — Sickness — Thought Forms — Pain — Focus —
Healing — Stress — Anger — Needs — Recognize Your Needs.

Yours   13

Your Choices — Your Name — Your Birthdate — Vibratory Energy —
Your Cycles — Your Parents — Your Family — Your Genes — Your
Acceptance —Your Best — Your Awareness — You Are Perfect —
Your Freedom — Your Transition — Your Salvation — Others'
Transition — Your Divine Unfolding — More Awarness — Conscious
Choice Transition — Comfort — Your Life Review.

Awareness   21

Hitler and Others — Resolution — Reincarnation — Bible Edited —
Release Fears — Gas Explosion — Broken Elevator — Boat/Swimmer
collision — Car/Truck Collision — Live Joyously — Accepting Yourself
— Your Labels — Your Self Talk — Increase Your Awareness —
Challenge Your Beliefs — Stop Labeling — Weather Awareness —
Expanded Awareness.

Joy   31

Suggestion — Love Yourself — The Bottom Line — Basic Question.

Part II
The 9 Chances

Explanation of This Section   35
Life Path Number — Your Birth Name — Your Lessons — More Insight to You — The Basics — No Regrets — Good Help — Increased Awareness — Parents — Check List — Let Go — Can You Wait?

Chance Number 1   43
Universal Meaning — Life Path — Birth Month Effect — No Pain, No Gain — Parents' View — Selective Choices — Your Focus —Children — Males — Females — Responsibility — Power Struggle — Irrational Expectations — Needs — Exceptional Chance — Rewards.

Chance Number 2   51
Universal Meaning — Life Path — Birth Month Effect — No Regrets — No Pain, No Gain — Sensitive Examples — Thoughts Create — Followers — Sharing — Students — Female — Children — Options — Exceptional Chance — Insight — Drive.

Chance Number 3   61
Universal Meaning — Life Path — Birth Month Effect — Spiritual You — Recognize Your Needs — Your Goal — Your Awareness — Both Chances 3 and 7 — Students — Children.

Chance Number 4   67
Universal Meaning — Life Path — Birth Month Effect — Students — Caution — Children — Both Chances 4 and 5 — Exceptional Chance — Thoughts Create — Your Awareness — Experience With Awareness — Another Exceptional Chance — Insight — Drive — Applied Idealism.

Chance Number 5   75
Universal Meaning — Life Path — Birth Month Effect — Children — Adults — Caution — Students — Parent Awareness — Both Chances 5 and 4 — Both Chances 5 and 7.

Chance Number 6   79
Universal Meaning — Life Path — Birth Month Effect — Students —
Willing Responsibility — Insight — Your Rights — Special Awareness
— Your Aura — Thoughts Create — Children — Caution —
Exceptional Chance — Insight — Drive — Selfless Service.

Chance Number 7   85
Universal Meaning — Life Path — Birth Month Effect — Students —
Children — Both Chances 7 and 5 — Both Chances 7 and 3 —
Spiritual You — Insight to Aloneness — Caution — Transfer Fears —
Ultimate Fear — Negative Attraction — Release Fear — The Green
Book — Insight to Prayer — Get Ready — Thought Forms Heal —
Insight to Healing.

Chance Number 8   93
Universal Meaning — Life Path — Birth Month Effect — Students —
Thoughts Manifest — Caution — Insight — Irrational Thoughts —
Erroneous Conclusions — The Frog — Children.

Chance Number 9   99
Universal Meaning — Life Path — Birth Month Effect — Most
Compatible — Law of Giving — Spirit of Giving — Metamorphosis —
Students — Challenge — Children — Special Significance.

Conclusion   107
The Equalizer — Responsible Parenting — Your Cleansing — Your
Healing — Go For It.

Inspirational Prayer

The Light of God surrounds me
The Love of God enfolds me
The Power of God protects me
The presence of God watches over me
Wherever I am, God is!

The Great Invocation

From the point of Light within the Mind of God
Let light stream forth into the minds of all souls.
Let light descend on Earth.

From the point of Love within the Heart of God
Let love stream forth into the hearts of all souls.
May Christ return to Earth.

From the center where the Will of God is known
Let purpose guide the little wills of all souls
The purpose which the Masters know and serve.

From the center which we call the race of all souls
Let the Plan of Love and Light work out.
And may it seal the door where evil* dwells.

Let Light and Love and Power restore the Plan on Earth.

....
*Embracing anything other than love.

Preface

You probably think there is room for some improvement in the quality of your life or you wouldn't open this book. Are you looking for insight into what life is all about and how to free yourself to live life to the fullest each day?

This is a book about your life and a system for helping you understand yourself and others. I wrote it to share the good news of your fabulous potential through your increased awareness (knowledge) of using positive self-talk and other techniques which promote stress-free living. A better world starts inside each of us. This book will encourage and inspire you to accept yourself, love yourself, and really think good thoughts about yourself. On that foundation you can then accept and love others. The word *accept* appears again and again here and is basic to the understanding of my premise. I mean for you to *accept,* embrace, and love yourself just because of who you are. You are God's child. Within you is divinity, your higher self, your God power, and this knowledge of who you are will help you "bloom where you grow."

Accepting others means to **observe** friends, loved ones, associates, and everyone around you and **experience** them as they are. Every time you are with someone, that person tells you strongly and clearly who he or she is and where that person is in maturity level. My use of the word *accepting* does not imply a judgment of approval or condonement and neither am I asking you to accept abusive, decadent, or oppressive behavior by others.

Having asked you to accept yourself and others by this definition, I intend to explain that when God's children know better they do better. Good news is beginning to unfold so please read on.

Accept You

If you don't think well of yourself, you have no capacity for thinking well of the people around you. You may feel threatened by other peoples' choices, jealous, angry, fearful, or other emotional states. Your emotional response to others may range from mild to very intense; but you can learn to let go of those feelings and live your life with joy.

When you accept yourself, you radiate that attitude to people around you and the effect is contagious. Good feelings about yourself spread to others like the ever-enlarging circles surrounding a pebble thrown into a pond. You will like the effect and love the new awareness of living your life happily *now*.

Choices

Do you want to feel good? You can choose to feel good about yourself or you can choose to feel miserable, unloved, or victimized if you want. You have choices. What are you choosing? Just because you felt a particular way for a long time doesn't mean you must perpetuate the feeling any longer. Every day is a new day. Start fresh. Do yourself a favor by curling up with this book. The good news is sure to follow. I am positive of that. I guarantee it.

Abraham Lincoln said, "Most people are about as happy as they make up their mind to be." He was referring to a universal truth. Happiness is your choice, your responsibility to make yourself as happy as you choose to be. **Happiness comes from within.** It comes from what you tell yourself about what you perceive in your life. Wisdom is the awareness to recognize that choices you make have the possibility of creating happiness or unhappiness.

Perceive, Believe, Feel

Throughout this book, I use the words perceive, believe, and feel. The meaning of these words needs to be explained so we will communicate clearly. To perceive is to observe with any of your five senses and make an evaluation or judgment based on what you tell yourself about this observation. Perceive implies a value judgment by you consciously or subconsciously.

Perception always limits and filters your view of life. Your perceptions are actually illusions, but they become your beliefs and are firmly programmed into your brain computer. Perceptions quickly become beliefs. Your receiver brain cannot distinguish between what actually happens and what you tell your brain has happened.

Observations about happenings in your daily life cannot be true in the absolute sense, because as soon as you make decisions about what occurred, what the incident means, if it is good or bad for you, or any other judgment, you alter and limit the experience. And yet, you put this perception into your brain computer and it remains there as a belief.

Your thoughts about *any* thing program your brain computer. Your body functions as a feedback mechanism, which gives you feelings. You then say you feel whatever range of emotions you are feeling. Beliefs become so strong by reinforcement they seem automatic to you when you simply react with emotion; but the thought must come first to feel anything. Everyone has "ups and downs," but what you tell yourself about what occurs makes the difference in how you feel. Where you get into difficulty in your feelings, and aren't sure why, is when you program a belief at a subconscious level and you don't know it is there.

Proof

I know my simple, direct method of explaining about the condition we call life is effective because I have shared this information with literally thousands of people since the late 1970s and received enthusiastic feedback of positive results. What I share with others really helps them see themselves, their lives, and others in a beautiful way.

The information in this book is based on sound universal truths gathered from many disciplines and presented in logical sequence. The spiritual values discussed do not oppose the basic premise of organized religions as far as I'm concerned. I actively participate in groups representing both spiritual and religious interests and have done so for many years.

I want to give you enough background information to convince you of the validity of the material but not get sidetracked by details that make lengthy, complicated, or technical explanations. This book is not intended as a comprehensive study because it doesn't need to be. My book is easy to read, to understand, and to apply. It explains how you might look at your life in a more appropriate way and let go of the old beliefs that kept you unhappy or resentful.

What You Want

Some ideas may seem contrary to your "belief system" (as the word belief was defined). Some ideas may seem contrary to what you believe your organized religion teaches. The ideas are universal truths and do not reflect the ideas of any one group of people, denomination, or creed. Other ideas may seem completely new, unusual, weird, bizarre, or interesting depending on your frame of reference at the time you read this.

People usually look for something specific in the material they choose to read, whether consciously aware of the process or not. Agreement is often what they seek. If the material reinforces your belief system, you may think this book is totally acceptable. If you don't agree with the material you may feel anger at the author, or you may lose interest and refuse to read any farther; but you lose an opportunity to consider another point of view. I believe we always find whatever we look for in our daily living because of our mindset, attitude, or point of reference. The following story dramatizes my point:

The Woman at the Well

A woman at the well in a small village was approached by a man who introduced himself as a newcomer to the area. He inquired of her, "What kind of people live in this village?" The woman asked him, "What kind of people live in your former village?" The newcomer replied, "They were unfriendly, critical, and kept to themselves. We had nothing in common." The woman replied, " I think you'll find the same is true here."

A second man approached the woman at the well before she filled her vessel. He also was new to the village. "What kind of people dwell here?" he asked. Again, the woman responded, "What kind of people dwell in your former village?" "Oh, they were wonderful people, helpful, friendly, and accepting." The woman replied, "I think you'll find the same is true here."

What do you look for? What belief system do you want to reinforce? Is it possible that you have trained yourself only to read or listen for agreement? Would you be willing to put aside any tendency you might have for judging and labeling and just read the basic premise for understanding? Open yourself to experiencing ideas you may enjoy pondering and from which you may find answers for your life. See where the ideas in this book come from before you make any decisions about the information.

What You Can Expect

The title of this book usually evokes the questions "How did you decide on that specific number?" "Why nine chances?" "Why not an even ten or some other number?" The answer is nine is symbolic of *all* the aspects of our humanness. Nine includes all the numbers needing to be experienced according to the system of understanding yourself which I will share with you.

9 Chances to Feel Good About Yourself consists of **Part I Explanation of Life** and **Part II The 9 Chances** for easy handling of the information. The Explanation of "Life" provides all the background to understand the basic premises, what is life, why are you here, how to think of yourself and others, how you accept the opportunities you attract, and much more.

You will learn to understand who is in charge of your life, where "problems" originate, and what "the secret" is of feeling fully alive and loving your life. You will consider spiritual values you can apply immediately and easily. Free yourself to live a joyous, positive, dynamic, and rewarding life. Be sure to read the entire **Part I** to become more accepting, compassionate, and feel better about yourself. The message is so clear and both **Parts I** and **II** work together.

Part II The 9 Chances is a system for determining specific, personal, predictable aspects of yourself and describes how to determine which Chances apply to you, loved ones, associates, employees, and others in your life. This system provides personalized insight into specific aspects of your life and others' lives which helps you understand yourself, what lessons you came into this life to learn, your special interests, and your relationships. Self-understanding is a key to living life more effectively. This part may be read selectively or in its entirety. Repetition of information is for a reason. People are usually not consciously aware of ideas presented only once. Ideas need to be repeated approximately six times to create an increased awareness. Spaced repetition is there so the ideas are recorded and your consciousness is raised.

Can you feel happy with what occurs in you life? Do you want to think even better thoughts about you than you do now? Well, here is your chance. In fact, *9 Chances to Feel Good About Yourself.*

A Daily Affirmation

The Creator in me fills me with Love, directs my life to
Light, changes all past to Light, changes my genes to
Light, changes me to be free to express Light, Life,
Love, Mind, Truth, Energy, Joy, Beauty and Peace.

Part I
Explanation of Life

Ours

Our Energy Source

Let's start at the very beginning. A creative energy source exists. We are proof of this. Flowers, trees, rocks, air, water, everything comes from a creative source. I find difficulty in applying one word to identify this incredible energy in its enormity and all-encompassing scope.

Some people label creative energy the Source, Light, Love, Nature, the Force, or God. I am comfortable using the word God. However, I don't think of God as a puppeteer who pulls our strings, puts adversity in our path, helps us get a new car, or win the lottery, and then waits to punish us when we "die." I don't believe that is God's nature at all.

I don't think of God as He or She, but for my mind to conceive of an energy and discuss it without assigning a gender is hard. Please bear with me in that respect.

I think of God as the "Is." God encompasses all creation. Everything else exists as an illusion or a perception. God manifests pure love. God epitomizes good. God has always existed and always will exist. God always exists because nothing can be destroyed. Everything in the world is matter that can only change from one form into another.

Our God Nature

We are all part of God. We are "chips from the block" if you want to think of our source in that manner. I think of our relationship to God this way: if I take a teaspoonful of water from the ocean to analyze in a chemistry lab, the chemical content is identical to the ocean. The teaspoonful of water is not the ocean, but it is identical to the ocean. We are identical to God. We are not God, but we are identical to God. We are created in God's image. So, we have always existed and always will. God doesn't just love "good" children. God loves us all no matter what because we have always been part of God.

Our Reality

We exist as part of God and God's gift to us is our Free Will. We function as co-creators with God in this life. We create our own reality. Because we have free will, everything about our life is a choice we make consciously or subconsciously. Health, happiness, economic status, sickness, insanity, all components of our life come by our choice. Nothing ever occurs as an accident or a coincidence. A reason exists for everything we attract. The reason is not always consciously known. We don't always understand, but we are always at the right place, at the right moment, to experience whatever is in our best interest. We unfold at our divine level and experience what is appropriate and helpful for our growth.

The very thing bothering us, burdening us, or perplexing us each day is the exact situation we attracted for our own growth. God isn't "doing it" to us. The economy isn't responsible for what we experience. Our parents aren't at "fault."

We know at our God level (our higher self level) what we need to experience in order to progress and to learn what we came into this life to learn. We don't seem to learn from our perceived successes because they feel terrific and we just go forward about our life.

We learn from situations, or people, when we feel perceived stress or pain because we hurt. Physical symptoms get our attention. We think a better way must be found and we start looking for it. The end result is an opportunity to analyze, rethink, and learn something.

Our Brain Receiver

How do we create our reality? We create with our thoughts. Thoughts are electrical impulses that create form. Thoughts have to come first before anything happens.

We know our brain is a physical part of our body. Doctors know where our brain resides in our body. However, our brain actually serves as a receiver that we input with our thoughts (consciously or unconsciously) and the brain receiver processes thoughts to manifest in our body and beyond. (I say beyond because that's why prayer is effective.) The final computation may be to feel depressed, mad, sad, happy, euphoric, a migraine, an aching back, and so on. I purposely combined emotional states and physical conditions in the last sentence because that is how your brain functions. Emotional states become physical symptoms.

Your brain does not question what you feed it, it just obediently processes all incoming thoughts. Your brain does not know the difference between truth and what you tell it is truth.

Well, how is inputting possible if your brain is just a receiver? Aren't thoughts created in the brain? Good question. I'm glad you're still with me. The best evidence says your mind programs your brain and that your mind exists outside your body. Think about it. Sometimes, people have been declared brain dead (no electrical impulses emitted) for several minutes to an hour and are able to recount they were completely aware of everything happening around them during this time. They knew what was said, what was done for them, and many other details. The mind is part of a higher consciousness.

Biofeedback works because your brain functions as a receiver. In this technique you may imagine (visualize) your hand in a bucket of warm water; and you imagine the water bubbling, swirling around and between your fingers and feel your hand getting warmer and warmer. The thought comes first. Then scientific measuring devices confirm your hand is several degrees warmer than before.

The mere suggestion of a lighted cigarette touching the skin of a person in a hypnotic state programs the brain to create redness, pain, and eventual blistering when in fact no cigarette exists. Hypnosis, visualization techniques, and biofeedback are effectively used tools in every aspect of your life whether you are consciously aware of them or not. You can reprogram your brain receiver with these fabulous tools and your brain obeys.

Prayer

Prayer is powerful because thoughts create. Be careful what you pray for, because you will probably receive it. I don't pray for a person to live because I don't know what is best or appropriate for the person. Pray for a person's highest good, and trust that divine order prevails.

Prayers do not need formal organization. Your very thought can heal someone else. I think of prayer for healing as a kind of spiritual jumper cable of my energy added to the other person's energy and needed because of temporary depletion of theirs due to stress.

When you pray, pray as though your concerns are already accomplished because that shows ultimate faith. Here is an example:

Dear God, thank you for Sue. Thank you for her perfect health. Thank you for her feelings of being loved. Thank you for her affluence. Thank you for her healthy ego and for the perfect White Light that surrounds, enfolds, and protects her for her highest good. And this is so.

Problems

You may think I am saying, "We only learn from our perceived problems." For something to be a problem you have to first perceive the person or situation as a problem, otherwise it just is.

Eliminate the word "problem" from your vocabulary. If you perceive your life is filled with "problems," you have to "work on your problems." You have to feel heavy, burdened, and all sorts of perceived negative emotion. You might hate to get out of bed in the morning because of the perceived "problems" you face. Your perception of problems drains your energy.

Opportunities

Change the word "problem" in your brain receiver to "opportunity" and you free yourself to see each day as filled with adventure, challenge, and "opportunity" to experience interesting, exciting situations that are all good for you and part of your divine unfolding. You could even bring a sense of humor to daily living experiences. Your energy flows in the most powerful way and you know you are fully alive to experience each present moment with joy. You can throw the covers back and bound out of bed with this kind of awareness.

What a difference in the way the chemistry in your body feels by changing that one perception. You can actually feel the difference inside of you. Test it for yourself. Go back to the above paragraph where I talk about problems. Then come back to this paragraph about a day filled with opportunities. Can you feel the difference in your body because of the difference between negative and positive thoughts? Your heightened self-awareness makes lemonade out of lemons. Your perceived stumbling blocks can really be stepping stones.

Live in the Present

What fun to have a new day to start, every twenty-four hours. You need only live each present moment one at a time. There is no need to be hard on yourself by clinging to the past with guilt, blame, regret, resentment, or bitterness. There is no need to worry, stew, or fret over things in the future.

When you worry, you energize a picture of something you do not want to happen. You actually attract the situation you fear the most. Surely you didn't realize how electrically charged thoughts can create. Picture in your mind a safe return, a healed arm, a loving reunion, or whatever concerns you.

Cop-outs

Removing the word "problem" from your vocabulary can help you see your life in a better way. The phrase "I have to" is another one to eliminate along with "I can't," "I should," or "I must," "You should," "I'll try," "I don't have time," and "If only."

Using the phrase "I have to" leaves you feeling like someone else pulls your strings; that you are not in control of yourself; that you are not responsible for yourself; and you often perceive yourself as a victim. You might end up with a "Pity poor me" attitude when you continually say, "I have to clean today, I have to go to the bank, I have to meet Brett for lunch." Change the "I have to" to "I want to" or "I choose to." Then you feel that you control you, and you accept responsibility for your choices. You don't really *have* to do anything.

When you understand the creative power in words and realize you have choices, you feel much better about yourself by taking responsibility for the fact that you "want" to or you "choose" to do such and such. Using the words "want" and "choose" channels the energy flow in your body most efficiently.

Eliminate the phrase "I can't." That is a cop-out and leaves you feeling helpless and victimized, again. You demonstrate a reluctance to take responsibility for yourself with that statement whether you realize your intention or not. People hide consciously or subconsciously behind a phrase like "I can't." Change "I can't" to "I don't want to" or "I choose not to." Those are honest statements.

Assume responsibility for your choices. You deserve the right to decide for you.

Using the words "I should" or "You should" creates another victim position and usually creates bitterness and resentment. "You should do such and such" puts the other person on the defensive immediately. Stop using "shoulds" and free yourself to feel better than ever.

The phrase "I'll try" is a cop-out to avoid saying "yes" or "no." Be honest and straightforward, and stop using the word "try." How do you "try" to lift a book, for example ? The task is impossible. You either lift the book or you don't lift the book, right? Eliminate this word from your vocabulary.

"I don't have time" is another cop-out. You have twenty-four hours in each day just like everyone else. You really mean, "I don't want to do a particular thing with my time," so honestly say that. Accept responsibility for yourself. You have a right to allocate *your* time, according to *your* priorities. You don't need to defend how you choose to spend your time. Accept your right to do that and own it consciously, honestly. Your energy level increases with each of these steps.

More Cop-outs

"I can't afford it" is in this same catagory. You afford the things you want to afford. Recognize that and take charge of your life so you feel good. You absolutely create your reality by all of these words, and the resulting feeling in you by the use of these words. I am not being picky. These words are electrically charged and they do manifest.

"If only" is also eliminated because the words refer to old news. Those words always deal with the past, with regrets, and with water already over the dam. Let go of all "if onlys" and know that you learned a lot through whatever you experienced. The situation was something you attracted anyway, and everything you experience is part of your divine unfolding.

Life with Our Body

We are not our body, our body is simply our vehicle in this life. We are a body, mind, and spirit and what happens in our body is influenced by the other two. Look for a psychological component behind physical symptoms. This outlook is called an holistic approach to life from *holos,* Greek meaning whole. The condition we call Life is actually a classroom. We choose to take on a body and come here to experience, learn, and grow.

I believe we exist always as a soul and we take on a body. A body helps us develop our awareness faster at this level by acting as a feedback mechanism for us. It gives us symptoms and acts as a barometer to alert us when our thinking is out of line. Our body tells us when we experience disharmony, and if we have this long enough or intensely enough our body manifests dis-ease.

Thoughts Manifest

Your body serves you very well. You want to keep your body healthy by the nourishment or fuel you feed it. But what you feed your brain receiver in the way of thoughts, which then manifest as health or disease in your body, is a million times more powerful than food you eat. The brain functions as a pharmacy in your body when you think a thought.

Thoughts are electrically charged and they do manifest in your body. That point is so profound, I want to elaborate to be sure you understand. This book could be called *9 Chances To Think Good About Yourself* because that is where a feeling starts. Feeling good about yourself is the result of how you first think about yourself. Be sure you understand how that works.

Whatever you think manifests in your body. Your perceived negative thoughts about a person or situation are all processed and contained within yourself. For example, if you perceive a person or situation as a "pain in the neck," you may manifest this in you and develop a stiff neck.

If you (consciously or subconsciously) perceive you have to bow to another person's authority or whatever you make your authority, you may start to carry stress in your knees and eventually develop physical symptoms in one or both knees. Sometimes symptoms occur very quickly, sometimes slowly. The onset of symptoms depends upon how intensely you program the thoughts into your receiver brain.

Sickness

Germs and bacteria are in our environment all the time. Why aren't we sick *all* the time? When you hold a thought that is not loving, you feel stress. Stress depresses your immune system and you open yourself to disease. I am not saying this is bad, it just is. You need to know how your thoughts manifest in your body so you can change any debilitating thoughts to allow healing to take place. (**Chance Number 7** includes additional insight to sickness and healing.)

Thought Forms

The thought "I want to pick up my pencil" produces chemistry instantly . You don't have to direct each muscle, tendon, or neuron to contract or elongate. You just think the thought and the chemistry (immediately produced) allows the complicated process to work easily.

If you believe someone cut you off in traffic and you choose to outrage yourself, what intense, immediate chemistry might you produce? Certainly, blood pressure can elevate substantially, heart beat increase, muscles tighten, hands feel sweaty, stomach tighten and so on. Your anger manifests in your body.

The thoughts "I don't want to see this room messy anymore" or "I hate to see my parents growing old" implies stress to your eyes. "I don't want to hear anymore arguing" or "You're fired" or an impressionable person being told "You never listen well" can produce stress that manifests in your ears. Clogging your emotions can clog your arteries. Perceived emotional hurts become physical hurts and pain. When you allow other people's remarks to "eat away" at you because you take the remark personally, you have dis-eases that eat away at your bones or tissues.

Pain

Physical symptoms indicate a need for us to analyze our thoughts when we experience disharmony or dis-ease. Perceived pain and suffering have nothing to do with God. We create our reality. We have to perceive we are suffering, or that something is painful, for pain to manifest in our body. We create our pain and suffering and not God, our spouse, our employer, the economy, or anything or anyone.

Our body tells us loudly and clearly how unhappy, down, and depressed we feel when we tell ourselves what we perceive as negative thoughts. Even though we may label a person or situation as terrible, horrible, tragic, or unfair, we can always find a way to change our negative perceptions to positive. When we change our thoughts, we turn our life right around and we feel good.

Focus

Every rose includes a thorn. Will you choose to focus on the rose, and feel love and warmth and harmony in your life, or will you chose to focus on the thorns? Remember the story of "The Woman at the Well" on page xii. If you look for thorns you will surely find them. You will feel self-righteous, bitter, critical, resentful, judgmental, and you may want to organize a protest march to place warning labels on roses.

We make ourselves a little crazy by the perceptions we choose to tell ourselves and the incidents upon which we choose to focus. Are you focusing on the rose or the thorn? You have a choice. The awareness of your focus applies to your perception of you, another person, or your perception of a situation.

Healing

Forgiveness plays an enormous part in healing and feeling good. You probably believe forgiveness means to forgive the person or situation you perceive wronged you. You believe it is someone or *thing* outside of yourself. That is a good place to start. However, to accomplish the release of old programming, you really need to forgive yourself, and accept what occurred for the learning situation it was. You are not forgiving yourself because you did anything "wrong," you are forgiving yourself for having wanted something so much from a person or situation you perceived you didn't get. That is the source of all anger, stress, and fear. Consider this insight carefully, for your benefit.

Stress

You create stress in yourself when you want something you believe you're not getting. You may label the perceived conflict a "Power Struggle" or a "Tug of War" with another person, or situation. When you change your negative perceptions to positive thoughts, you let go of your end of the rope in the "Tug of War," and the power struggle no longer exists. Your "problem" is not your husband, mother-in-law, some other person, or situation. Your problem arises from your inablilty to accept a situation over which you have no control. You are the only one over whom you have power. You cannot change another person or situation but you can release all of the stress by changing your thoughts.

Would you be reluctant to stop thinking a person behaves rudely, or someone let you down, or your step-children are spoiled rotten, or any other judgment? Do you think that would let the other person off too easily? Is your goal to be happy or is it to punish the other person and teach him or her a lesson?

Do you believe (think) happiness also creates stress? It can, if you *believe* it can. Happiness, laughter, and smiles release endorphins to promote wellness in your body if you experience them without limiting them by thinking that happiness is stressful, too.

Some people have a difficult time accepting happiness and success, because they are afraid they don't deserve happiness. We are all children of

God. God's children deserve the best of everything. Accept and enjoy the happiness you create.

Anger

Do you ever feel angry (hurt) with your loved ones? Your employer? In-law? Neighbor? Do you ever upset yourself when you perceive someone has ignored your wishes? Why upset yourself to the point of anger about something over which you have no control? You can only control you. Why would you even choose to create anger at yourself? How would your anger with yourself help in any meaningful way? Anger is a choice. You can choose a different response when you understand emotions result from thoughts. Why perceive anything in your life as something about which you upset yourself to the point of anger when it doesn't change anything? Anger allows an enormous drain of energy. Eliminate your perceived need ever to be angry. Changing your perception is easy to do if you think it's easy, and hard if you think it's hard. Be careful what you tell yourself.

You create anger in yourself when you want something you believe you're not getting. What do you want, specifically? How realistic is that? Do other people know you expect them to change what they think or do so you will feel happier? You set yourself up for disappointment when you want others or a situation to change because you think it's best for you. Do other people know exactly what you want or do you just hint?

Have you used accusatory statements like "You never write" or "You always work overtime" instead of "I would love to hear from you" and "I miss our time together"? Even if you clearly communicate your needs, are you realistic in expecting someone else will change to "make you feel more comfortable"? It is not realistic. It is irrational. Release people to be who they are.

Needs

If you expect other people to meet your needs, you will feel anxious, nervous, and fearful. When you learn to meet your own needs, you release the anxiety of hoping others will know what you want from them.

Suppose that people agree to change themselves "to make you happy." If you didn't feel "happy" before, will you really feel "happy" now? Isn't the irrational thought "If only so and so would do such and such then I'd feel happy," what you are telling yourself? Isn't there "just one more thing" you notice, on which you focus and about which you annoy yourself? Your mind set is, "When others change then I'll feel happy."

You want to choose to be happy *now*, because your happiness does not depend on others. Happiness comes from your attitude and mind set. You want to choose the thoughts that maintain happiness. You may think of happiness as love, the Christ Consciousness or many other labels, which have the goal of maintaining joy, peace, contentment, increased self-awareness, and a loving outlook within you. (Christ Consciousness is a spiritual title refering to a very high level of consciousness. The name Jesus refers to a highly spiritual male personality.)

Recognize Your Needs

You usually attract people who fill your perceived gaps, people who meet your needs and help you feel whole. When you recognize your perceived wants and needs and learn to be creative in giving yourself what you want from others, you then free yourself to come to others out of choice rather than out of need. That's the way life works the very best.

If you need appreciation, recognition, acceptance, love, security, or a hug, learn to give them to yourself through your positive self-talk. When you perceive your needs are met by others, that is "the cherry on top of the whipped cream." It is really pleasant, delightful and terrific. You may think of the experience as a compliment. If you make what others say or do regarding you the "Main Course," you always set yourself up to feel insecure, inadequate, or any emotion you have made a habit. Does that make sense to you?

A Thought

As you yearn to be free and to bring freedom to others, remember that no one is free until one is master of oneself.

As you strain to speak, be aware that the real in us is silent, that the language of the heart is the main thing; the spoken word is merely the interpreter between the heart and the hearer.

Yours

Your Choices

Many decisions are yours to be made as you consider an Earthly experience. Let's go back to the preliminary planning stage for your life on Earth and consider the process further. Because you are made in God's image, you have always existed and always will exist. So one choice you make is to take on a physical body and come into this life. You make the choice for a specific reason or reasons. You make many choices which you program into your brain receiver as an outline for your life. At your higher self level, you know the experiences you want and the most appropriate way for you to accomplish your goal.

This process is predestination only in so far as what you choose for yourself. You want to be sure certain items are included as givens so nothing is overlooked or side-stepped.

Your Name

One of your first choices is your name. Do you think your mother named you? Your grandmother? You actually chose your own name or inspired the person who named you to give you a name representing all that you encompass. Your name is truly your signature and brings a specific energy with it.

Your Birthdate

You also chose your month, day, and year to come into this life because that also brings a specific energy for you. Your parents may consider your birth accidental, or they might have planned carefully; but you planned and timed it for the most appropriate moment for you. You knew exactly when you wanted to enter. Your time of birth is no accident by you.

Vibratory Energy

Your particular name and exact time of birth are unique because of their innate energy. When I speak of energy, I refer to the fact that everything in the world is matter and that the matter is all electrically charged. Everything vibrates at a measurable rate, a frequency rate. For example, you recognize the color yellow because the molecular structure in yellow vibrates at a frequency you recognize as yellow. Red vibrates at a very different frequency. You know where to tune to your favorite radio station because you dial a particular frequency on your radio. Vibratory energy within and around a person is called one's aura. This condition is the personal vibratory rate of the individual and can be seen as colors around each of us.

The moon controls the tides of the oceans. Evidently, the moon vibrates at a frequency affecting water. Our body is approximately 85 percent water so we logically think the moon affects us, too. I believe it does. The other planets vibrate at frequencies affecting other aspects of our body. These vibrations do not control us, but they affect us.

Your Cycles

Do you notice incidents in your life occuring in cycles? You experience particular things for a while and focus on those; but then become aware you aren't in that arena any longer and you focus on different matters. I believe the energy in the planets keeps events in your life moving and progressing.

Your Parents

This choice may surprise you. You chose your particular parents for reasons of your own. Choosing your own parents can sound incredible and bizarre if you encounter the information here for the first time. Hundreds of people under hypnotic regression have verified this. They said, "I knew who my parents would be." Even children who have been adopted said, "I knew my biological mother was just my vehicle into this life and I knew who would adopt me." Pretty fascinating, isn't it?

At your higher self level, you choose the parents you believe are the most appropriate parents for you. If you feel anger, resentment, or bitterness toward your parents it is a sure sign you attracted a learning situation within your family. This situation was necessary for you to experience for your growth. You will emerge stronger and wiser because of your perceived struggle. If you hadn't selected those specific people, you would have selected similar types because of your desire to stretch yourself and grow in wisdom in that area of your humanness. You want that type of situation and think it is in your best interest. If your parents feel very comfortable for you, that probably isn't where you want to learn a lesson.

Your Family

Let's continue with your choices when you are deciding to come into this life. I believe you choose your spot in the family, because that brings a family dynamics with it. You choose to be an only child, the baby, the first, or somewhere in the middle for a reason.

You learn a lot because of your position in your family. If you have siblings, you may each experience the same family in many different ways because of economic, physical, mental, spiritual, or political attitudes that may be present at one time and not at another.

Your family and your spot in the family functions as a living laboratory of experiences and opportunities for you to learn. You have no need to carry any resentment or bitterness in connection with your family because you chose your family. They are part of your growth and development. Accept your family.

Your Genes

Another choice you make is your packaging. You choose your physical make-up from your huge genetic pool. There is no one way to live a life. You can choose to come into this life blind, deaf, with a withered arm, or with a physical symptom label such as Downe's Syndrome, mentally impaired, or any other way. If you really want to be noticed you can choose to come in with red hair, seven feet tall, or in the body of a dwarf. You can come in looking like Elizabeth Taylor or Elephant Man.

If you want lots of love and attention you can choose a sickly, frail body to have people really concerned about you, hovering about you, and taking special care of you. You choose what packaging serves you best. Your physical appearance or the vigor and stamina of your constitutional makeup only matters in so far as how those choices best serve your need to experience life in the manner you perceive is in your best interest.

If you decide someone is too tall, too fat, has thighs too large, has a nose too pointed, is ugly, or anything else, you waste energy again. Let go of judgments and labels. We are all God's children and packaging is not a contest. Your body is simply your vehicle through this lifetime.

Your Acceptance

You are here learning and experiencing, and the main lesson to learn is stop judging and labeling so you can accept and love. Just enduring your life and getting through it somehow is not enough for you. Until you learn to live your life with joy, you haven't learned what you came to learn.

You feel more compassion for everyone (yourself included) when you accept people as they are. You could choose to experience life as a "derelict" or a "dowager." What does it matter, as long as you progress and learn to live life with joy? Money and health do not assure happiness or joy. You can feel miserable and fearful with or without money and health. Whatever you experience, however you look, whatever your occupation, or lack of it, is a choice you make. We are all here to learn and grow, and we all exist on different rungs of the same ladder. We all do the best we can at any given moment; when we know better, we do better.

Your Best

Are you choosing to feel guilty now because you realize everything about your life is a choice you make at some level, and that *you* keep yourself sick, unhappy, or miserable throughout the years? Are you creating anger in yourself because you perceive I made some outrageous statements? Are you really mad at me, or are you mad at yourself for choosing negative thoughts (fears) you now perceive restrain you? Well, you have no logical reason to be hard on yourself because you always do the best you can at any given moment. For you to do otherwise is impossible, because of your receiver brain. "Garbage in, garbage out" in computer talk.

You program your brain receiver with thousands, if not millions, of thoughts and ideas of your own and with many of the thoughts and ideas of those around you. So at any given moment, your brain receiver kicks out the most appropriate behavior or response for you based on the total information you processed into it. You always do the best you can, but when you know better, you can do better.

Your Awareness

Be very selective in what you choose to allow into your brain receiver. Thoughts are not just idle meanderings. Thoughts are energy that creates.

What kind of messages did you hear about yourself? What kind of labels and judgments were suggested for you? You may have mistakenly computed thoughts and emotions of your mother's while you were in her womb, and thought they were your thoughts. If your mother was angry, you might have thought she was angry with you. If your mother had fears and insecurities, you might have acquired them as your own. Free yourself from old belief systems, self-doubt, or self-recrimination to accept and love yourself and also to accept and love others.

You Are Perfect

Just in case I haven't convinced you that you do the best you can at any given moment, here's one more example which may help:

Suppose you decide to bake a cake from a prize-winning recipe. This is a delicious sounding, attractive-looking cake. You follow the recipe exactly as printed. When you taste the first bite, you find it tastes as salty as brine because of a tiny error in measuring the ingredients. The cake is not perfect for the original recipe but perfect for the ingredients used.

The use of the word perfect refers to a process innately created for us, and we cannot operate any other way. You are perfect at any given moment based on the electrically engineered design of your brain receiver. The word perfect validates present moment behavior. I am not using perfect in the classic sense.

Your Freedom

Are you perceiving if you accept these ideas you will become a robot-type person who doesn't feel anything; and you wouldn't want to be like a robot? That thought is irrational. The fact is you free yourself to feel more of what you choose that creates love and joy and harmony, and less of what creates pain and misery within you. You create your own reality. Are you creating it lovingly, or bitterly? Which do you choose? Your perceptions of reality are always your choice.

Your Transition

You know now about your free will to choose every aspect of your life. What about death? I think of what we call "death" as a revolving door. Transition is a better word because the dead are not dead. The wonderful spark or energy that is you or your loved one remains intact as always.

We are an energy (soul) and we take on a body. You are not your body. When you make your transition, very little happens. You shed your body (physical form) that served as a vehicle and a barometer, and you are still a spiritual form. You are God's child in a form which has always existed and always will exist.

Your Salvation

We perceive we are separated from God and we need to find salvation. In reality, we have always been "saved" because we have always been part of God. Salvation is a myth of organized religions to control congregations through fear. God loves us no matter what occurs because we are an integral part of God.

Others' Transitions

Are you wondering how the perceived loss of a child, spouse, or significant person in your life could be thought of as anything but horrible and tragic? Of course you *miss* that person because they were a *big* part of your life. They were a big part of your daily routine, the way you celebrate holidays, or a big part of where you invested your energy. You almost always perceive that as a loss.

You feel pain as long as you perceive that transition is horrible and tragic. When you accept the fact that your loved one made his or her transition and release them to be in their new form, the pain is gone. Transition is also a choice. Your loved one lives every moment that is appropriate for him or her and then departs the physical body. No accidents, no coincidences.

Your Divine Unfolding

I believe children who make their transition *chose* an abbreviated life for themselves. I believe they are here for a reason. They impact someone's life, or many people's lives, accomplish what they had in mind, and go on to their next adventure.

I grant you a person's transition often seems like an accident, but the "accident" serves as a catalyst or facilitating means for making the transition. Within the person is always a higher reason and a divine unfolding taking place.

I feel such comfort in thinking about life this way. There is no need to run the whole gamut of emotions such as even feeling anger at first with the person, for "leaving me." That is a very common, normal feeling, but the person doesn't leave you, abandon you, or leave you in a mess on purpose, or any of the other perceptions on which you choose to focus. No rational reason exists for you to take the transition personally.

More Awareness

When I was about eight or nine years old I acquired a cat, Fluffy. I really loved that cat. When my cat "died" I was so mad at the cat for "leaving me" and I was mad at God. I thought God had taken my cat. I was unconsolable in that matter for a long time.

Now when I "lose" someone close to me I am aware of grieving for my own needs regarding that person, because I really understand and accept this was a choice appropriate for them. Many of your choices are made at subconscious levels of your brain, and this is usually one of them.

Conscious Choice Transition

There are people in Tibet who have reached a highly developed state of awareness that allows them to *will* themselves into transition at a conscious choice level and depart their bodies for the next life experience. Isn't that interesting? If this aspect interests you, much information is available on what we commonly call death, or near death experiences, and out of body experiences.

Comfort

Knowing a spiritual reason why people "die," and that "dying" is just returning to a purely spiritual form comforts me enormously. I certainly don't believe "death" is the worst possible condition that could ever happen to a precious person.

I am puzzled by devout people belonging to organized religions and believing in an "after life" who still act as though dying was to be avoided by all means. A statement such as "Oh no, I don't want you to consider mountain climbing, you might get killed" is an example.

Earthquakes, plane crashes, floods, tornadoes are all possible facilitators for people making their transition. You are always at the right place at the right time to experience whatever is in your best interest.

Your Life Review

God's nature is pure love, and God doesn't just love good children. God loves all of His or Her children. God is not waiting to judge you and punish you. God is not going to say "Remember last week on Tuesday afternoon? Shame on you, you really could have done better." That is ludicrous.

At your higher self level, *you* review your life. You know if you accomplished everything you came to accomplish. If you did, you may very well choose to go on to your next adventure, in the spirit world.

When you review your life, if you perceive a few more aspects of your humanness you want to experience to a fuller measure, you can choose to take on a body and come into an earthly life again.

Another possibility is that you learned all your lessons and yet you choose another life to make a wonderful contribution to help someone else who is planning to come into a life. Because of your possibly enlightened state, you can inspire, guide, and teach a particular person, or even a group of people. I believe you might have another physical life experience for various reasons, but the choice is yours. God's gift to you is your free will.

Awareness

Hitler and Others

What about rapists and murderers? How do they fit into this? And what about Hitler? Well, they are God's children, too. The Christ Consciousness dwells in everyone and everything and there is no one way to live life. They learn and grow by their experiences but probably not in ways you and I would choose. However, when they know better they will also do better. Everything occurs for a reason. Everything we experience is ultimately for our growth and development.

At his higher level of consciousness, I think Hitler agreed to play the role that he did. He made an incredible impact in raising the consciousness of everyone who ever heard his name and story. Much of the world was shocked and horrified by his acts and took a giant step forward.

Surely, Judas must have agreed to play the role he did also. Jesus knew one of his desciples was to betray him and he knew it was Judas. Judas seems to have been part of the divine unfolding.

Resolution

Believing there is always a reason for everything that happens seems so loving and comforting. Believing every occurrence is for our ultimate good, helps us accept, experience, and love, knowing that perceived unresolved incidents will always be balanced, eventually. Remember the old phrase "It will all come out in the wash"?

Reincarnation

The above phrase does embrace the idea of reincarnation. I believe reincarnation makes a lot of sense and explains some unusual occurrances that are otherwise unexplainable. For example, Bach and Mozart's extraordinary talents in music at two or three years of age.

Some people with pronounced obesity respond so poorly to professional treatment for weight reduction that alternative methods such as hypnosis are sought. Through this means of introspection, a lifetime in which the person died of starvation is sometimes uncovered. When the ancient memory is released as "old news" and no longer appropriate for the current life, the person is often able to lose weight effectively for the first time. Difficult phobias may be better understood in this context. Phobias are sometimes released by looking into previous incarnations for their source.

Reincarnation may explain homosexuality as convincingly as any other explanation from medical or psychological studies and possibly even better than those. No discipline of the scientific community has definitive reasons for homosexuality. I do believe it is a choice and the person chooses it for a reason.

On the other hand, I am not fanatical about whether there is or isn't such a process as reincarnation. What does it really matter? Now that you know you are responsible for all of your choices, you have no need to use whatever you perceive occurred in a previous incarnation as an excuse for your behavior in this life. That would be a waste of your energy, and another cop-out.

What does it matter what you experienced last week or five years ago, or that you might have felt unloved as a child, or even what you attracted in a previous incarnation? Those experiences are all in the past, they were all for your ultimate growth, and you have no need to carry resentment or blame because you created it anyway. Every day is a new day. Live and experience your present moments.

Just because you may perceive you were unwanted, unloved, or suffered yesterday doesn't mean you must set yourself up to maintain that position today, tomorrow, and always. When have you suffered enough? Let go of the perceived woes of the past to free yourself to live with love and joy today. Letting go is so easy to do if you think it's easy. You make it very difficult to let go if that is your belief. Be careful what you tell yourself.

Bible Edited

The Bible actually contained many passages referring to reincarnation until it was edited in 425 A.D. by Emperor Justinian I and his wife, Theodora. Every passage referring to reincarnation they found was removed because they perceived their subjects could not be controlled as well when they believed in reincarnation. They thought they removed them all but they overlooked three passages which are still in the Bible.

Release Fears

If an ancient memory carries over into this life in the form of a phobia, for instance, you might want to release it. Your goal is to free yourself from all labels, judgments, and fears because your computer brain keeps the old program in force in your life if you don't free yourself from it. The programs (beliefs, perceptions) you adopt become restrictive and limiting, and you put yourself in a smaller and smaller box. You reduce the quality of your life and your opportunities to grow.

Through a thought such as "This is bad for me" you allow fears to develop. Your thought to your brain receiver creates the fear you feel in your feedback mechanism, body. When you reinforce this type of thought many times each day, over many areas of your life, you greatly shut-down your experiences, and vegetate.

Probably the strongest fear for many people is the fear of "dying." When you are free of that fear because of your understanding of "death," you have no need to perceive fears in anything. You are free. It is a joyous feeling.

Time Examples

Our transition is accomplished when we are ready and not before. I believe at our higher self level, the time to make our transition is always our choice. We live every moment appropriate for us to live, and then we make our transition by shedding our physical body.

Parachutist Paul Harvey, ABC syndicated network radio news, tells of a man who fell 7,000 feet because his parachute failed to open. He landed on an asphalt driveway, shook himself a bit, got back in the plane and jumped again. (His only comment was his wife would kill him when he got home.) It wasn't his time.

Gas Explosion Three elderly people were asleep in a beautiful brick home that was built like a fortress, even bolted to the foundation. A gas explosion in the middle of the night caused a fire which took the firemen nearly three hours to extinguish. The house was blown four inches off its foundation and most of the bricks were blown off the exterior but the three people walked out of the destroyed home without even experiencing burns. It wasn't their time.

Broken Elevator A young woman named Robin lived and worked in a huge high-rise building in New York. One day the elevator in the building malfunctioned. She was between floors with two companions. They all agreed to climb out of the elevator and notify the superintendent to repair it. What the three decided to do seemed practical, safe, and logical.

The first man climbed out as planned. Robin was next. As she was about to secure herself on the nearby platform her purse bumped a strut, just enough that she missed her landing spot. She fell seven floors to her "death." The next man climbed out without incident.

Robin was a very intelligent woman and had exceptional physical agility. She performed ballet for many years. She might have caught another support and experienced a broken arm or leg or whatever. It was Robin's time and the elevator was the facilitator.

Boat/Swimmer Collision A priest was swimming alone in a large lake at 7 A.M. A young man and his friend were on the lake to waterski at the same hour. The priest was killed instantly when the skier's boat ran over him.

Consider the circumstances involved here. The first rule of safety in swimming is "Never swim alone." Waterskiing rules require a watcher in the boat in addition to the driver and skier. Rules were violated by both participants; but how could they find each other in order to collide on the big lake? The boater didn't purposely want to terrorize the priest, he didn't even see him. He only felt the impact.

The priest might have lost a finger or a hand and survived; but it was his time and he made his transition. The dynamics of this situation are for an ultimate reason at a higher level of consciousness between the priest and the boater.

I know of many stories demonstrating this point and you probably do too. Here is just one more.

Car/Truck Collision A couple expecting their first baby very soon were sitting at a traffic light on a road empty except for one approaching vehicle. An intoxicated truckdriver drove through the intersection and into their car. All three were killed instantly.

The couple might have driven two miles an hour faster or slower and avoided that particular light. They might have been the second car at the light. There are many collisions every day and people walk away from them unhurt. Sometimes a baby is delivered alive from a mother who has been dead for an hour or more. A flat tire or a forgotten purse would have changed the outcome entirely.

There was a reason why that precious family chose to make their transition then and together. I don't know the reason. I don't have to know the reason. I accept that they know why and they have shed their physical bodies together. It was their time.

Live Joyously

I have an agenda in mind for myself and the resulting manifestation feels so good in my body that I want to share the ideas with you. I want to share what I know is good news. My agenda is to live my life with joy, and I encourage you to do it also.

You may repeat the following affirmation as often as you like and the pro-gramming of it in your brain computer will manifest beautifully in you:

I have no other desire but to know my higher self. I am not my body, I am not my "problems," I am not my emotions. I am in touch with my Godlike self.

Accepting Yourself

How does one live life with joy? You accept yourself, love yourself uncondi-tionally, and feel good about you so you free yourself to respond rather than to react. You feel so good about yourself because of your positive self-talk that when someone around you is angry, for example, you don't take their behavior personally by reacting (to the other person's behavior) yourself.

You have every right to be you, and you accept that others have the right to be who they are. Whatever anyone says about you reveals so much more about them than their words say anything about you. You have no need to perceive another's statement as a judgment against you. Love yourself so thoroughly that you are free to be magnanimous with others.

Accept and love yourself even if you perceive yourself overweight, too short, too tall, pushy, sloppy, impulsive, impatient, inefficient, thoughtless, sickly, or any other label you use.

Your Labels

Any of the words in the columns that follow may be chosen to label a person or situation positively or negatively, depending on your perception. Maybe read that last sentence once more, it is important. I am saying any of the words could be used by you and manifest a happy feeling or a down feeling depending on your intent when you use the word. They all require a judgment made by you. Remember, my goal is to increase your awareness to free you from labels which keep you restricted. Do you identify with any of them?

accepting	determined	fool	impulsive
aggressive	dimwitted	forgiving	inflexible
ambitious	dishonest	formal	informed
angry	disobedient	friendly	insensitive
assertive	dispassionate	funny	inspiring
bitter	distrusting	generous	intelligent
bossy	doer	genius	intolerant
calculating	dogooder	glad	intuitive
calm	dove	go getter	jealous
caring	dry	goer	joy
casual	dull	gossipy	judgmental
cheat	dumb	grouchy	lazy
clever	easy going	guiltless	leader
co-operative	emotional	guilty	liar
cold fish	failure	half fast	limp
compassionate	fast	harmony	listless
compulsive	fastidious	hateful	loner
controlling	fat	helpful	loose
crazy	ferocious	honest	loud
creative	fighter	hot tempered	love
critical	flamboyant	humorous	mad
cross	flexible	hurt	manipulative
demanding	follower	ignorant	meddling

melancholy	possessive	sensitive	uncaring
methodical	positive	sharp	uncontrolled
neat	pity	short	uncooperative
negative	practical	sickly	uncreative
nervous	private	skeptical	undemanding
non-assertive	proud	skinny	underweight
non-judgmental	public	sloppy	unemotional
obedient	punctual	slouch	unfeeling
obsessive	pushover	slow	unforgiving
old	pushy	smart	unhelpful
opinionated	quick	sneaky	uninformed
orderly	quiet	sourpuss	unintelligent
original	remorseful	strong	unperceptive
outgoing	resentful	stubborn	unpleasant
overweight	reserved	stupid	unpossessive
peacemaker	responsible	success	unsuccessful
perceptive	rich	tall	visionary
perky	rigid	thoughtful	warhawk
picky	rowdy	thoughtless	weak
placid	sad	tight lipped	wimp
pleasant	sarcastic	tolerant	wishy washy
pleasantly plump	scheming	trusting	witty
pompous	selfish	trustworthy	young
poor	selfless	unaccepting	yuppy

Your Self-Talk

If you selected any words to describe you that you perceive as negative (a flaw or weakness), you will think to love yourself unconditionally or any other way is very difficult. Can you think of how all those labeling words can possibly be used in a positive way? Does that increase your awareness by thinking about your perceptions (beliefs) regarding those words?

If you believe you have negative traits, your belief makes the letting go of that posturing impossible for you to accomplish. You cannot feel good about yourself as long as you cling to that belief. In fact, your self-talk has a tendency to escalate instantaneously in intensity which really creates unhappiness within you.

For example, you may start with the thought "How can I hold up my head and face people as much as I have to learn?" Your second thought may be "I am a real dummy and a failure much of the time." You could easily arrive at the thought "Life is a bummer" faster than it took me to describe this process. Your thought must come first to produce the chemistry to create the feeling you then manifest in your body.

Increase Your Awareness

Where does reality really exist then? The absolute truth is you create it. Reality is your perception of what is occurring. I use the word "perceive" many, many times to help you clearly understand that reality is your perception of reality, your belief of reality, and is actually an illusion. In fact, you may perceive in an irrational manner that traps you and keeps you feeling unhappy.

I want to help raise your awareness level of what you tell yourself. I hope the repetition of this word will help challenge your beliefs of what you "perceive" reality is.

Challenge Your Beliefs

Are you willing to challenge your beliefs? Read through the following list to awaken your awareness, and free yourself in the process. So, what is your goal? What do you want? You have many choices:

- Do you choose to perceive yourself happy? Do you believe you would be like a Pollyanna and she is unrealistic?)
- Do you choose to perceive yourself a victim? (Do you believe you are a doormat for others, and people take advantage of you?)
- Do you choose to keep making yourself sick? (This choice gets you out of something, or gets you something you don't know how to get any other way.)
- Do you choose to perceive yourself as poor? (Do you believe you probably don't deserve a better life or that money is evil? Do you want someone else to take care of you?)
- Do you choose to perceive yourself a worrier? (Do you believe that good people "should" worry to show love and compassion, and those who don't worry are cold and unfeeling?)

- Do you choose to continue making yourself angry when your anger does nothing to change anything? (No one is making you angry. You choose to be angry or it couldn't happen.)
- Do you still choose to perceive people are rotten, and keep setting people up to reinforce your belief?
- Do you choose to perceive others let you down?
- Do you still choose to perceive the world owes you something, and you were cheated?
- Do you still choose to perceive your mother didn't love you? (Are you punishing yourself by maintaining that position, by withholding love from yourself?)
- Do you choose to perceive you were abused when you were little? (Are you abusing you, even now?)
- Do you choose to perceive you need attention from others?
- Do you really want to continue saying "I am cold natured," "I have trouble breathing," "I hate snow," "I get mad when...," "I'll gain weight if I eat that," "I never get a good putt," or whatever negative thought you tell yourself?
- Do you choose to keep punishing your husband for not sending flowers or remembering a day each year that is special to you? Would you perceive you are happier to continue to berate him and undermine your relationship than to meet your own need by sending flowers to yourself? Which gives you more satisfaction? Why?

Stop Labeling

Whatever is happening, just is. Weather is just weather. It's not a huge source of stress unless you make it stressful and important to you. And people are who they are, period.

If you judge that something or someone is rude, unfair, awful, tragic, inappropriate, or any other judgment you tell yourself it is bad for you. Then you wallow in the trap of self-pity, anger, resentment, or any other victim position. Taking daily experiences personally has nothing to do with experiencing reality and, in fact, is really a cop-out to avoid confronting and learning from the present situation, which you attracted anyway.

When you feel depressed, you depress your immune system; and the resulting trauma in you does nothing to change what actually occurred. It only hurts you. Experience whatever is occurring without labeling it and you will get through it beautifully.

Weather Awareness

Practice this awareness with your perception of the weather for a few days. What do you tell yourself about sunshine, rain, clouds, humidity, heat, or cold? Probably a whole range of thoughts on this topic. Your thoughts program you to feel certain ways, depending on certain weather conditions. You are so skilled at it that your corns, arthritis, and other physical symptoms know when to act up, because of weather, based on what you believe about weather.

Free yourself. Weather is just weather and you have no power to change it. Why upset yourself about something you have no power to change? Do you depress yourself on gray days? Where is "gray means gloom" written? Gray is just another color. It doesn't have to be bad. What's wrong with clouds?

Is rain always bad? It's just water. Rain helps plants grow, rain can alter terrain, rain can collect to the point of being called a flood. You are here to experience and grow. If you experience a flood, that's what the flood is, an experience. If you label it bad, does that change anything? You just feel bad. You can feel bad if you want to because you have that choice; but if your goal is to feel good, be aware of what you tell yourself about a flood.

Could you reach a state of awareness where you feel happy while experiencing a flood? Feeling horrible doesn't clean up the water any faster. Cleaning up is just a procedure.

Expanded Awareness

Do you dread Mondays because of what you tell yourself that Monday means? You don't have to see Mondays that way. You could change the picture in your mind, and change the resulting feeling about starting a new week.

You could feel like a "phony" at first because you are doing something different and you "Don't feel right," "I don't feel like me," "It's scary," "I'm not as unhappy as I usually am so this must be bad." Are you judging and labeling again? If you want to change your feelings, then change your thoughts.

Joy

Suggestion

How do you see yourself at this time? I choose to see myself as a totally, unconditionally loveable, happy child of God, and experiencing my life with joy and blessings beyond my wildest dreams. That is my goal, my agenda. How does anyone really do that? I know that I can strive toward that each day, by experiencing without judging.

We are here to attract situations with which to relate and challenge ourselves. This is often labeled ups and downs. They are the opportunities from which we grow toward our goal of "graduating" from this Earthplane classroom we call Life.

Love Yourself

Are you thinking this idea of how Life works sounds fairly logical actually; but you're still wondering how to live it? Live it by accepting and loving yourself and others. The idea is so basic, so easy. Then why does anyone make it hard and complicated? Because you don't love yourself. You were told "You are selfish to think of yourself" and "You are conceited to think well of yourself." The "Me Generation" acquired a "bad" name. You were taught "Good deeds you do for others is all that counts."

Jesus taught that we are to love our neighbor as we love ourselves (Matthew 19.19). Start by loving yourself, and then you have love to give to others. If you don't feel good about you, you are so busy holding the perceived remaining fragments of you together because you think others are taking pieces out of you, you have nothing to give. A better world starts in each one of us, a better world starts in you.

Was there ever a time in your life that you loved yourself? Even a little? At certain times, maybe? Aside from all the things that might have been said to you, could you think back in your life to a time when you can see yourself as absolutely loveable, no matter what? Can you think of a picture of you in an old family album when you are so young, precious, innocent, and vulnerable that you could agree you are totally deserving of love, unconditionally? In fact, totally loveable?

Go back to an age young enough that even if you burped milk on your daddy's suit coat, tracked mud across the kitchen floor, you thought your nose was funny or you had a patch on your little shirt, you could still put your arms around that precious little you and give you a big hug.

Are you picturing yourself? Is it summer or winter? What are you wearing? You are holding the picture of you in your mind; you could accept that little person you are thinking of and visualizing now; and put your arms around yourself and love you as you are, unconditionally? Right?

I want you to know that precious, loveable little person is inside of you. Be good to that child. Take good care of that little person and know you are God's child. We are all God's children. We are all sisters and brothers.

We separate ourselves from the divinity within us by our judgments. Judging is an irrational action to engage in when we know better. We can choose to stop judging now.

The Bottom Line

If we are to live our lives in the way Jesus and other spiritual teachers have demonstrated for us, how would it be possible to do that if there was no order or reason whatsoever to the events in our lives? I will not perceive God, whose nature is pure love, allowing His or Her children to be "eliminated" by a train crash or to "catch" a debilitating physical condition for no reason. I think the condition we call Life would be the poorest experiment or joke that a loving God could perpetrate on His or Her children. I think it would be intolerable. I would not choose to participate.

Basic Question

The logic of my thinking is you are here, and you are going to live Life. Are you going to live it lovingly and joyously or miserably and bitterly? There is comfort and potential for a fabulous life, as I have described it to you. I believe this is the way it works. If I am wrong, the worst thing that happens is you think you had a wonderful life. Where is the harm?

Love is Come Again

When our hearts are wintry, grieving, or in pain
Thy touch can call us back to life again.
Fields of our hearts that dead and bare have been
Love is come again, like wheat that springeth green.
(a French Carol) by J. M. C. Crum

Prayer of St. Francis of Assisi

Lord make me an instrument of Your peace;
where there is hatred, let me sow love;
where there is injury, pardon;
where there is doubt, faith;
where there is despair, hope;
where there is darkness, light; and
where there is sadness, joy.

O Divine Master, grant that I may not so much
seek to be consoled, as to console; to be understood
as to understand; to be loved, as to love;
for it is in giving that we receive,
it is in pardoning that we are pardoned,
and it is in dying that we are born to eternal life.

Part II

The 9 Chances

Explanation of This Section

The Chances are nine aspects of your humanness or nine lessons to experience so you fully learn about life. They are nine different energies you learn to handle. I refer to them as Chances but they may be called opportunities as well.

This part of the book requires your active participation to determine which Chances apply to you personally, or whomever you want to understand. Unlike other arenas of active participation, you won't need special shoes for this. Each of the Chances begins with information on the Universal Meaning, Life Path, and Birth Month effect.

The Chances explain what you want to accomplish with your life. This is called your Life Path. They also tell you the personal lessons you came to learn, about your personality, and about cycles in your life. Are you thinking "Wait a minute, how can this possibly work?" (Are you still open to reading for information and not necessarily agreement?) The system is based on your name and your birth date. The wonderful part of the method is you don't even have to believe in the idea for the process to work. Keep reading. What you read will probably amaze and delight you.

The numbers one through nine assigned to the Chances have universal, symbolic meaning. If you aren't familiar with the scientific meaning inherent in numbers, you might easily dismiss *The 9 Chances* as worthless, or meaningless. I would have thought the idea ridiculous and absurd at one time myself. I only valued analytical reasoning, Ph.Ds, and academic authorities, period. If you couldn't prove a statement to me in a science lab, I wouldn't allow you to "waste my time." Well, I now acknowledge the existance of an unseen dimension which I know is powerful, real, and loving. (And it has a sense of humor.) The unseen world is an enormous part of life.

My experiences in pre-marital counseling, marital counseling, bereavement counseling, wayward children counseling, and other areas are based on this method as a tool for understanding the individual. Thousands of counseling sessions have thoroughly convinced me of the accuracy. I would be a fool to deny the validity of this method when I know how well this tool works.

As I explain the process, write the information you will require on a piece of paper or a 3x5 card. The completed information tells you which Chances to read.

Months are referred to by their chronological number in determining your Life Path. January is one because it is the first month of the year, February is two, March is three, and so on.

Life Path Number

First, write the number of the month, day, and year of your birth.
Example: If *November 14, 1958* is your birth date write it:
11-14-1958
Add (from left to right) each single number all the way across.
Be sure to use all four numbers of the year.
Don't abbreviate 1958 to '58.
1+1=(2)+1=(3)+4=(7)+1=(8)+9=(17)+5=(22)+8=30 total.
30 is the total, but use only single numbers.
Add the two numbers across, to reach a single number:
3+0=3
3 is the Life Path number for this date.

Life Path numbers may be considered lucky numbers.

Write the words Life Path and your personal Life Path number on the card so you will have them for easy reference.

Repeated Numbers (Exceptional Chances)

The repeated numbers 11, 22, 33, 44 and so on to 99 are significant as total numbers, before reaching a single number. The repeated numbers greatly intensify the single number that follows. The meaning of the single number is found in that number's section. If your total is a repeated number, write that number and then write the single number on your card. I refer to these particular numbers as Exceptional Chances. If you have repeated numbers, look for your combination of numbers in the Exceptional Chance section of the individual Chances later in the reading.

Example:

January 12, 1962

1-12-1962

1+1=(2)+2=(4)+1=(5)+9=(14)+6=(20)+2=22 total.

22 is the total and a repeated number.

Write that number, and then add the two numbers

to reach a single number. 2+2=4

Write the single number on the card.

22/4 is the Life Path number for this date.

Example:

February 18, 1975

2-18-1975

2+1=(3)+8=(11)+1=(12)+9=(21)+7=(28)+5=33 total.

33 is the total and a repeated number.

Write that number, and then add the two single numbers

to reach a single number. 3+3=6

Write the single number on the card.

33/6 is the Life Path number for this date.

Two More Exceptional Chances

The number 13 and the number 19 are significant as a total number, before reaching your single number. Write that number and then write the single number on your card. If you have one of these numbers, look for your combination of numbers in the Exceptional Chance section of the individual Chances later in the reading.

Example:
October 10, 1901
10-10-1901
1+0=(1)+1=(2)+0=(2)+1=(3)+9=(12)+0=(12)+1=13 total.
13 is the total and an Exceptional Chance.
Write that number, and then add the two numbers across
to reach a single number. 1+3=4
Write the single number on the card.
13/4 is the Life Path number for this date.

Example:
October 1, 1943
10-1-1943
1+0=(1)+1=(2)+1=(3)+9=(12)+4=(16)+3=19 total.
19 is the total and an Exceptional Chance
Write that number, and then add the two numbers across
to reach a single number. 1+9=10 1+0=1
Write the single number on the card.
19/1 is the Life Path number for this date.

Is that clear? Do you know how to determine what your number is now? Did you remember to write your Life Path number on the 3x5 card?

Your Birth Name

I arranged all the rest for you in an easy to follow sequence based on the exact name you were given at birth. Your name and your birth date are the outline of your life. Your name is actually your preparation for life. Your birth date is what you do with your life.

If a clerical error was made in your name at birth, don't use that. Print the name you believe was intended for you on the 3x5 card. Don't use a confirmation or baptismal name which was added later. Correct spelling is imperative. The letters in your name are significant. They indicate many things about yourself.

Your Lessons

You come into a life and first attract the situations and experiences that help you learn the lessons you came to learn. When you have confronted and learned all of your lessons, you don't need to continue attracting those same kinds of situations. The energy you used in those areas is freed to be directed toward your Life Path.

The lessons you came to learn are indicated by certain letters of the alphabet which may be missing from your full name. You may have *all* the letters one ever needs. This means you probably learned *your* lessons but you are here for other reasons. You may be here to inspire and teach or further enhance and *enrich* your experiences. This may be a kind of Ph.D. type life (piled high and deep with experiences for you). Maybe you came to enjoy this beautiful world and fully smell the roses. You are definitely here for a reason and you know what it is at your higher self level.

You will use the letters in the name on your card to check the list on the first page of each Chance and determine which lesson or lessons you came to learn. Write on the card the number or numbers of the Chances which apply to you.

More Insight to You

Underline the first letter in your first name on the card. This is the cornerstone of your personality. Use that letter to check the list on the first page of each Chance and determine which Chance applies to you. Write the number of that Chance on the card.

Write the name of the month in which you were born. Your birth month affects you from 0 to 27 years, approximately. Write the number of the day on which you were born. Your birth day affects you from age 28 to age 54 approximately. Write the number of the year in which you were born. Your birth year effects you from age 55 approximately through the rest of your life. (Do not reduce your birth day number and year number as you did your Life Path. That is not necessary here.) Locate the Chances which contain your month, day, and year. Write the number of those Chances on the card.

Be sure to finish reading the rest of this section for more information and then read those Chances which include the letter, month, and numbers you have written on your card.

The Basics

At your higher self level, you chose to attract situations in which you experience any or all of the Chances 1 through 9 to a significant measure in your life. If your life hadn't contained the actual situations you experienced, the situations would have been something similar because that is the arena of learning you perceived was appropriate for you and in your best interest.

You learn a lot with your specific Chances. Remember, you don't learn by your perceived successes. Successes feel so good you just go happily onward. You learn by incidents which catch your attention because you feel upset, angry, depressed, hurt, or other perceived negative emotions. You analyze what you attracted and look for a better way of experiencing them the next time.

In your eagerness to demonstrate proficiency in learning the Chances you may "overdo it," go to "extremes" in certain areas, or be very intense in certain areas until you are convinced you learned. Then you can relax some of the energy you put into any particular Chance and maintain a more moderate position.

No Regrets

You can easily carry resentment, bitterness, regret, blame, or hurt because of the unhappiness you perceive while experiencing your Chances. You know now that releasing old thoughts is in your best interest, because it was all a learning experience for you and part of your divine unfolding. You attracted those opportunities because you create your reality.

Good Help

If you don't think good thoughts about yourself, you make it difficult for you to apply yourself in confronting your Chances. You may incapacitate yourself in your ability to confront the opportunities you attract because of perceived insecurities or perceived lack of love. You may almost shut yourself down.

How do you start to think good thoughts about yourself? If you need help, there is wonderful information for you in the section *Love Yourself*. Read the loving approach to accepting yourself again now, and then come back to this page.

Increased Awareness

Remember, none of the situations you attract are innately terrible, horrible, awful, tragic or unfair unless you perceive them as such. They just are. A learning opportunity exists in anything you think is heavy or burdensome, and there is a reason for everything you have chosen to attract. You feel emotion and pain when you resist accepting the situation. The pain is gone when you accept reality at a factual level and not a perceptual level. This does *not* mean to accept abuse or oppression of any kind. Abuse may well be a learning situation but you must recognize that you *always* have choices and move on with your learning. Don't get "stuck" in any lesson.

Parents

Parents who know what their children want to learn can relate to them in a more harmonious way and help encourage growth in specific areas. Parenting in an overly concerned or insistent manner is unnecessary because children are enormously creative in meeting their own needs. They learn and grow in their own way.

Parents need not be heavy handed or punitive. The use of moderation, common sense, and love encourages and reinforces activity in specific areas. At least avoid working against any needed Chances. The personality and character traits that your infant or toddler demonstrates are really who they are, period. The individual emerges very early.

Check List

Do be patient with yourself. Accept and love yourself. Believe good things about yourself. When you have the awareness to do this, be sure to complete the process by being patient and loving to others. A better world starts with you.

People do the best they can at each moment, so there is no need to upset yourself by what others are doing, or not doing. Others have a right to be who they are and to list priorities for themselves. Why upset yourself about something you cannot control such as others' behavior, weather, traffic delays, congested waiting lines, mechanical break downs, or the Detroit Tigers losing. Your upsetting yourself does not change anything. You are only hurting you.

Let Go

When have you punished yourself enough by your *old* thoughts? When have you suffered enough from old self-talk? Pain and suffering from your thoughts are created by you. Your thoughts create your reality. God is not doing that to you. God's nature is pure love. Have the awareness to let go of old thoughts which hurt you, so you stop punishing yourself.

When you confront your Chances, process the information, and apply the knowledge learned from them, there is no need for you to keep attracting the same type of "problem" again and again. If you seem to do that, there must be something more for you to understand. Think about it, because as soon as you learn your lessons you free yourself to put all of your energy into your Life Path.

Can You Wait?

You are ready to read the Chances. Be sure they include the ones containing your Life Path number (that probably is the most important Chance), the lesson or lessons you want to learn, the cornerstone of your personality, your birth month, birth day, and birth year which you wrote on your card.

If you have the same Chance apply to you three or more times, you are very focused in that area of learning. That aspect may mean harmony, determination, accomplishment, goals reached because you chose energy at that level for a reason. You may have a tendency to compulsion, obsession, intensity to extremes, stubborness, fixed, and rigid behavior because you may be really hard on yourself. Those perceived negative words certainly don't imply you are "bad" if someone lebels you with one of them. You know by now that none of the words are innately terrible or awful. Whatever you do and however you do it is all a learning experience for you.

Reading the Chances selectively as suggested above will help you be more accepting, compassionate, and think better thoughts about yourself. Reading *all* the Chances whether you believe they apply to you or not, will help you see the entire picture. We are all so much more alike than we are different that you may identify with all 9 Chances and think they all are helpful. Consider reading every word so you won't miss a thing.

Chance Number 1

If you have any aspects in the following list, this Chance applies to you.

1 Life Path number
19/1 Life Path number
No **A, J,** or **S** in your name (lesson)
Only one **A, J,** or **S** (lesson)
A, J, or **S** the first letter in your first name (cornerstone)
Born in **January** or **October (0-age 27)**
Born the **1st, 10th, 19th,** or **28th** day of any month **(age 28-54)**
Born in l900, **1909, 1918, 1927, 1936, 1945, 1954, 1963, 1972,**
1981, 1990, 1999, or **2008 (age 55-on)**

Universal Meaning

One symbolizes masculine energy in a psychological sense, what society perceives the masculine energy represents. One is leader, original, independent, take charge, be the boss, initiate for yourself, stand on your own two feet, new beginnings, courage, ambition, emerge as your own person, decision maker, loner, and progressive thinker.

Life Path

You probably lead, direct, boss, originate, pioneer, reform, produce, trail blaze, or have an "Indian Chief" position. If an obvious way of doing something exists, you find a far more interesting, unique way of accomplishing your goal. You are a self-starter and initiator.

Birth Month Effect

(0-27 years approximately)

If you were born in January or October you probably had a person or situation in the early years of your life whom you perceived dominated you. You may have felt you were confined, restricted, or restrained by one or both parents, an older sibling, or grandparent living in your home.

You came into this life like a Rolls Royce engine and you thought someone wanted to put a throttle on you. You might have left home early or married early because you didn't feel free to be yourself as long as you lived under that person's jurisdiction or in that household.

You perceived your parent or whoever restrained you was the "problem." Your problem was not that person. Your problem was your unwillingness to accept the person you could not control.

No Pain, No Gain

Because of this perceived pain you grew stronger and stronger. You stretched yourself, expanded your awareness, and learned a lot. If you had people around you who were very relaxed and always pleased with your choices, accepting, and so on, you wouldn't have learned the lessons you wanted to learn. You would have needed to be more and more creative in attracting other situations, where you would stand up and initiate for yourself.

Parents' View

If you thought you were dominated by one or more of your parents, another consideration is your parents did what they perceived good parents "should" do. They did the best they could based on their level of development. Your parents might have believed themselves irresponsible, if they had done less than they did. Your parents thought they knew what was in your best interest. They really wanted you to become an effectively functioning adult. They might even have been fairly inadequate in parenting skills by some people's standards; but I believe you chose them for a reason. You eventually emerged as your own person and were capable of taking charge of your life.

Selective Choices

Do you accept the idea your parents did the best they could? That parents are absolutely perfect at any given moment? Think of your favorite recipe, again. You know when you combine the ingredients and follow the directions carefully, the end result will be the same delicious dish you always enjoy. If you change one ingredient, the dish may not still be your favorite; but it is a perfect dish for the ingredients used. You, your parents, everyone is perfect at any given moment.

Think again of your brain as a computer, storing all of your experiences, beliefs, thoughts, and choices. The most appropriate way for you to behave is the only way possible for you at any given moment, based on what you place in your wonderful computer brain. You want to be very selective in the thoughts you choose to put into your brain because your thoughts create. Thoughts are electrically charged, and they do manifest in your body in the form of feelings. You must have a thought first, before anything happens in your body.

Depressed thoughts manifest so you feel down and fearful; and you depress your immune system with perceived negative thoughts. If programmed strongly enough or often enough, you may experience physical symptoms or dis-ease.

Positive self-talk maintains your sense of self-worth or self-esteem and frees you to behave in rational ways. When you accept and feel comfortable with who you are, you *choose* your response to others at a rational level, rather than react to others.

Your Focus

Accept and love yourself with unconditional love, and accept and love the people around you for the good dwelling inside each one of them. Every rose has a thorn. Do you focus on the rose and feel love and beauty, or focus on perceived thorns and become critical, fearful, and judgmental? Are you organizing a protest march against thorns? Do you demand a warning label on roses? The Christ Consciousness is in every one of God's children. We are all God's children. We all live the best we can and when we know better, we do better. Be patient and good to yourself and to others.

Children

Children missing A, J, and S are here to learn all of the qualities described at the beginning of this Chance. You can help them by giving them an opportunity to decide which of two outfits to wear, or which book to read at bedtime, which game to play, which toys will be shared, or which day to go to the zoo. Offer opportunities for them to lead and decide, within appropriate boundaries.

Males

A man without A, J, and S in his name is here to learn to take charge, lead, be the boss, and so on. This life may be his first incarnation as a male. He may want a position of dominance, because he believes he needs to demonstrate proficiency in this Chance. He may attract many situations where he is in a position to make decisions. He may go to perceived extremes, because this role is so new to him. He is learning to be the "Indian Chief" for the first time.

A man whose name does not have A, J, and S who perceives some adversity, may suffer a great deal and believes that going forward and initiating for himself is difficult. If he believes his security and self-worth is severely undermined, he may perceive standing on his own two feet again is extremely hard to do. Men with this aspect often follow a "family script" in vocational choices; and if the job terminates for reasons not of his choosing, he may perceive he was emasculated and incapacitated. His lack of experience in initiating for himself and poor background of decision making skills may contribute to his possibly "giving up" and not looking for employment again.

Females

A woman who is strong in Chance Number 1 energy and missing B, K, and T in her name is very much like a male mind in a female body. She is one strong, capable female. She is probably her own person and handles her life independently. This life may be her first incarnation as a female.

Responsibility

If your name contains none of these letters, or if you have just one of them, you may think blaming others for what you are experiencing is easier than taking responsibility for your own role in whatever you attracted. This also applies to what you might perceive as accidents. You may look for a "too slippery floor," or a leg of a chair that was "out too far" that "caused your fall," and not accept that it was a "do it to yourself" project. There is no rational reason to focus blame on anyone or anything when you realize you create your own reality.

Power Struggle

When two or more people in the same family, office, committee, or team are strong with 1 energy, a power struggle could arise. A situation with many Chiefs and few Indians results. The OPEC sheiks may be an example. Two Chiefs together can feel like a "Tug of War" game. A Tug of War only exists until one end of the rope is dropped. That game is impossible to continue without two participants. For two strong people to be aware of the leadership potential present when they are together is helpful; and they can strive to channel the leadership in constructive ways so that *much* is accomplished. A commitment to recognize others' ability to lead, as well as your own, plus good common sense can produce a "think tank" of achievement.

If you are in a position to set up committees and chairpersons, it is helpful for the Chance 1 people (leaders) to have Chance 2 people (co-operative followers). Leaders need someone to boss and to whom they delegate details.

Two leaders in the same family have every right to disagree on ideas, choices, or anything else. They both have a right to be themselves and a right to their opinions and perceptions. If you exercise your rights, prepare yourself for the other person to have the same opportunity. Practice hearing yourself saying "We can agree to disagree on that because we see that very differently." There is no need to "step outside" (to fight physically) to settle differences.

Irrational Expectations

If you upset yourself because of what someone else said or did, you really want the person to change so you will "feel" more comfortable. Your expectation is irrational, and you set yourself up for the perceived disappointment you feel. Your expectations based on the thoughts you tell yourself about a person or situation create the "let down" feelings you perceive in your relationships. You really do it to yourself.

Release people to be themselves. For you to keep expecting them to be different than they have already demonstrated they are is irrational. Haven't they demonstrated whatever their pattern is many times? Are you unwilling to accept them as they are? Do you keep coming back for more disappointment with your expectation that they will be different this time and only discover the situation is just "Here we go again..."?

Needs

Leaders often attract subordinates, people who follow. They may often attract people who want to be dominated. In this situation both people have their needs met. The relationship may work very well until one of them outgrows that need or it works well as long as the self-talk dialogue is positive. But if one person moves on to a different position (grows), the other person may feel bitter, resentful, or victimized. The original relationship may breakdown (change) at this point.

Male, female relationships may be viewed in the same context. In some families, a male may dominate and in others, a female. If a breakdown occurs in the role each one plays, the relationship may not survive. This needn't feel like the end of the world. Needs may be met beautifully at first; but when one person grows through the original need, the dynamics can change. People can grow together during changes or grow apart. The determination of the commitment to each other or mutual love may be strong enough to maintain the relationship. Or this change may result in separation or divorce. You learned much with that person and you were attracted to them for a reason that is part of your growth and development. Don't tell yourself "My marriage didn't work," or " I failed in my marriage," or " I am a failure." Changes in needs may build a wall between people or build a bridge. Whatever the outcome, make the choice with love rather than with hatred, bitterness, or revenge.

Exceptional Chance

If you have any aspects in the following list, this Chance applies to you.

19/1 Life Path number
S the first letter in your first name (cornerstone)
Born the **19th** day of any month **(age 28-age 54)**
Born in **1918, 1927, 1936, 1945, 1954, 1963, 1972, 1981, or 1990**
(age 55-on)

If this applies to you, you came into this life perceiving you owe something to someone, a situation, or possibly to humanity. You feel an indebtedness and you really want to make it right. You want to wipe your slate clean and leave all of your Chances balanced, completed, repaid, and resolved.

In fact, you may want this life to be your final incarnation on the Earthplane. If you had a quarrel with someone and haven't spoken to them in some time, you will want to attract that person back into your life to "bury the hatchet."

This drive to attract people or situations with whom you have unfinished business could create some interesting, unique, or unusual situations. You may want to keep a journal if you have a flair for writing. You may not realize how unique some of these situations are because you are living it. You could think everyone's life is like yours, but others observing the experiences you have might find events in your life extremely fascinating, even good reading.

Rewards

This aspect could manifest another way, for example, if you give of yourself in a caring, loving way, a kind of "Cast your bread upon the water with no thought of return person," this life could include "rewards" for you. Some project you want to start may be accomplished with so little effort it almost seems to fall into your lap. When you give of yourself with no thought of return, you do receive tenfold.

Prayer for the New Day

Wonderful, wonderful, fortunate you,
This is the day that your dreams come true!
This is the day that your ship comes in;
This is the day you find Christ within.
This is the day you are glad to live;
This is the day you have much to give.
This is the day when you know the truth;
This is the day when you find new youth.
This is the day that brings happiness;
This is the day you will live to bless.
Wonderful, wonderful, fortunate you;
This is the day that your dreams come true!

Chance Number 2

If you have any of the aspects in the following list, this Chance applies to you.

2 Life Path number
11/2 Life Path number
No **B, K,** or **T** in your name (lesson)
B, K, or **T** the first letter in your first name (cornerstone)
Born in **February** or **November (0-age 27)**
Born the **2nd, 11th, 20th,** or **29th** day of any month **(age 28-54)**
Born in **1901, 1910, 1919, 1928, 1937, 1946, 1955, 1964, 1973, 1982, 1991, 2000,** or **2009 (age 55-on)**

Universal Meaning

Two symbolizes feminine energy in a psychological sense, what society perceives the feminine energy represents. You are a follower, helpful, co-operative, obedient, peacemaker, dove, tactful, diplomatic, considerate, nurturing, sensitive, accepting, receptive, good at time commitments and details, usually wanting a best friend, partner, or spouse because you like to work in tandem. You like to work through others to accomplish what you want to do.

You are a coachable person on a team, at home, in a parochial school, or in the military because of your willingness to follow orders. You are a welcomed member of any committee and influenced by your associates, so be selective in choosing friends. You enjoy comfortable surroundings for yourself and loved ones.

Life Path

You may be in the military, a nurse, a caretaker, assistant, companion, housekeeper, nanny, teacher, diplomat, sensitive artist, or musician. You may be on a sports team, team efforts of any kind, a board member, or in a partnership.

Birth Month Effect

(0-27 years approximately)

If you were born in February or November you may have been "mother's helper" with younger children. You may have attracted a situation in which you were the one to mother and nurture yourself due to particular circumstances in your home. Your role with your mother might have been reversed, because of family conditions. If your mother was invalid, alcoholic, or even if you were motherless in your youth that was not your "problem." Your "problem" was not the person you perceived criticized you, put you down, victimized you, used you, was insulting, rude, or witheld their approval of you. Your problem was your unwilingness to accept a situation over which you had no control.

No one except you has the power to make you feel any particular emotion. You alone control your emotions. Emotions are choices you make in how you will respond. Emotions become habit and ultimately a belief that when such and such occurs you automatically feel a particular emotional response. Emotional responses are learned, and so may be rethought and rechosen.

When you accept yourself and love yourself, you don't need to take things personally, or to look for "slights," or reasons to feel down. Why would you choose to feel down? When you feel good about yourself, you are more likely to take the next step and feel good about others, too. Why not? We are all brothers and sisters, all God's children. The Christ Consciousness is within every one of us. To live your life with joy, perceive the Christ in each person and each situation. Every rose has a thorn. On which part do you choose to focus? Your focus (viewpoint) is always your choice.

No Regrets

You may have developed resentment and bitterness because you perceived you were cheated by not having the childhood you thought you wanted. Have you been able to put aside regrets and "if onlys" you might have carried during those early years?

If you are a strong leader who is learning to follow, you may have developed stress or frustration because you perceive exactly what needs to be done but you are not in a position to demonstrate your talent until you experience this Chance Number 2. When you understand you chose to learn this Chance, the awareness certainly makes the situation easier for you to accept. You attracted those opportunities because you create your reality.

No Pain, No Gain

You probably perceive yourself as accepting and magnanimous because of your willingness to allow many viewpoints. Generosity in attitude is typical of 2 energy. Your strong trait may also be perceived as weak, if you believe others' viewpoints are judgments of you.

Because of the sensitivity of this energy there is a possibilty of setting yourself up to believe you were criticized or "put down" when people state their thoughts or beliefs. You have no need to consider a statement by someone else to be a judgment against you unless you have some unfinished business within you to examine, recognize, and release.

You may also set yourself up to believe you are a "victim," to feel you are being "used," or that another person was "insulting," or "rude." These labels are judgments made by you when you tell yourself negative things. You set yourself up to feel insecure, depressed, angry, hurt, insulted, put down, or criticized because of what you tell yourself about what someone else said or did. This outlook is commonly known as "Taking things too personally." You aren't thinking good thoughts about yourself if or when you do that.

Believing negative self-talk is a big drain of energy and totally irrational. The fact is that everyone has the right to make statements. Others have a right to their opinion and to be themselves. You have a right to your opinion and to be you. Accept this right for yourself and others.

The statements you make say much about you, and contain no power to do anything to me unless I play a part in the discussion by reacting to your statements. I would have to believe there was some truth in what you said about me, if I upset myself over the words you say. Otherwise, I would just listen calmly, knowing that I was still fine, relaxed, and lovable no mater what you just said or the way you said it. I would need to read something negative into your tone of voice if I upset myself over the way you say the words.

Assertiveness training is very helpful in learning techniques to help you handle situations in ways which allow you to feel good. Assertiveness doesn't train you to control others, that is impossible. You learn ways to change your thoughts, which changes your feelings. You are also learning that here, so read on.

Sensitive Examples

Taking things personally can be stopped when you are aware of the potentially vulnerable times and prepare for them. Put two or three of the following phrases that seem most helpful to you on a 3x5 card and carry the card in your shirt or blouse pocket. Keep it close by and handy to use until you have thoroughly learned to feel good about yourself.

The first time you are aware of an opportunity to use one of these phrases, it would relieve a potentially stressful situation and create a humorous scene if you pause, take the card out, and read aloud from it. You can say, *"Wait, wait! I have an answer for that!"* Wouldn't that be funny? I dare you to do it.

These phrases are helpful when you perceive other peoples' statements to be judgments against you.

Agree to Disagree

"We see that differently. We can agree to disagree on that topic." (Good to use with family.) You have a right to disagree. Having your own opinion is not "making waves" or being "unpleasant." You have a *right* to your opinion. You can calmly say this phrase, or duel to death to determine who is "right" and who is "wrong." Remember, your opinion isn't necessarily "right,' either. Your opinion is just that, your opinion but you have a right to it.

Clarify

"I'm confused," (slight pause) *"What specifically do you want from me that you think you did not get?"* (Good to use with someone you perceive in position of authority.) Making this statement is a way to clarify an issue, if an issue exists. This one may be repeated, effectively.

Agree

"You may be right, I'm really trying." (Good to use with a spouse.)

Pretty hard to argue with you when you already agreed. Even so, you may feel a need to repeat the phrase once more. This time, a little softer and a lttle slower.

Variation *"You may be right, you may have a point."* (Good to use with children.) You don't argue, defend, or debate with this statement and you really don't "buy it" either, because maybe they aren't right and they don't have a point. This one can be very effective.

Reflect

"You seem upset with me because of my opinion. Do you want me to change what I think so you will feel more comfortable?" The idea that I am expected to change because someone wants me to is irrational . I have a right to my thoughts and opinions. I have a right to be me. People frequently anger themselves because someone else's opinions or beliefs are not like their own, and they probably aren't consciously aware of what they are asking of the other person.

With increased awareness on your part you can say this calmly and lovingly, even with a quieter voice than you normally use. The effect often evokes a more rational outlook from the person upset with you; but don't expect it will work every time because the person may not understand your question. Your goal is to keep from taking other's statements too personally and this phrase really helps you do that. It works great.

Spoof

"You sound really upset with me. I guess I am a big disappointment to you." This is such an exaggeration it often gets an apology. You certainly don't believe what you have said, because you have a right to be you. Another person has no right to have expectations of you. When people do that, they set themselves up for the anger they feel. They are thinking irrationally.

Flippant

"You are so observant." (Good to use with family.) I always laugh when I say this one and tension is relieved.

Testing

"Oh, I guess you think I am a bad girl. In which corner do you want me to stand?" (Good to use with family.) Light-hearted response, and then you might ask what the person really wants from you.

Do any of those seem helpful? Choose the ones you think are right for you. Choose the ones you could say as calmly and sincerely as you possibly can (without feeling guilty or superior) or they probably won't have the effect you want. You may want to practice a bit, but don't give up. These statements can really help. Persist with these phrases ; they will help keep your awareness and they will become natural for you to use.

Thoughts Create

If you describe yourself as sensitive, you create some predictable physical manifestations. You may create "sensitive" skin, environmental "sensitivities," or be "sensitive" to certain foods. These are sometimes called allergies.

Followers

If you chose a strong Chance Number 2 and so has another person in your home, decisions may be difficult to make because you both want to follow. You have two Indians and no Chiefs. No need to blame each other for perceived lack of leadership ability. You chose the accepting, pleaser role for a reason. Use common sense and deal with it, lovingly.

Sharing

Many men are attracting this Chance now. As women take more responsibility for themselves and learn independence, men are developing their sensitive, nurturing side. We are moving toward a beautiful sharing of whatever roles we perceive males and females play. The "Me Tarzan, you Jane" mentality is disappearing rapidly. Children are reaping the benefit of two nurturing parents.

Students

If you are missing B, K, and T in your name, you are here to learn all the qualities described at the beginning of this Chance. You may have all the talent to be an Indian Chief, but in this life you want to learn to be the Indian. You want to put a restriction on your leadership ability while you learn to accept and follow. Having a best friend, companion, spouse, or business partner with whom to work would be right for you. You often find yourself in a position where you say, "If you just tell me what you want done, I will be happy to help you." You are in a position to follow a ritual, procedure, or rules.

Female

If you are a woman missing B, K, and T, this life may be your first incarnation as a female. You are like a male mind in a female body. You are a strong, independent lady who could resent learning to be submissive. Let go of any resentment, because you chose to learn this aspect of your humanness. No one is doing anything to you.

Children

Children missing B, K, and T could be helped by encouraging their co-operation with a list of family guidelines posted on the refrigerator and colorful stickers which they apply, when given permission, for rewards. They might help with the care of younger children, attend parochial school, or Montessori school. Encouraging this child to participate in sports that require coaching would be another way. Making a game of observing time commitments, praising attempts at developing patience, and so on could be helpful.

Options

Children may come into their life a little "pleaser," a "mother's darling," and accept the Chance Number 2 eagerly, even overdoing it until they learn it. Children may use this energy another way also. They may continue to avoid learning the Chance, because the ancient memory of their leadership ability is still close to their consciousness. Their thought may be, "It's my way or the highway." Their independent self is still wanting to take charge and be the boss. They may think to be helpful and co-operative just because their mother asked them was "giving in." And if they don't want to do what she asked, "I wouldn't be true to myself to agree under these circumstances." Children learn one way or another because there is a divine unfolding within them.

You may live in a foreign country where you are unfamiliar with currency, customs, and language. Being a minority in any living or working situation would help you learn the 2 Chance.

You may have a collection of some sort as a hobby or you may collect to the point of clutter and find it difficult to discard. There are many ways to learn.

Exceptional Chance

If you have any aspects in the following list, this Chance applies to you.

11/2 Life Path number
K the first letter in your first name (cornerstone)
Born in **November (0-age 27)**
Born the **11th** day of any month **(age 28-age 54)**
Born in **1901** or **1910 (age 55-on)**

If this applies to you, you probably are an experienced person with a definite mission in this life. You are on the practical Earthplane, but your consciousness is tapped into a much higher vibration. You are an idea person. Ideas come in you and through you that are so inspired, visionary, and idealistic. You surely are aware of this. Don't you sense things? You might describe yourself as intuitive, imaginative, perceptive, psychic, spacy, or creative. Do you trust your thoughts? If you pay attention to them and notice what you notice, the information will grow stronger and better.

Insight

If someone told you what you sense is not logical or practical, you might deny a beautiful aspect of yourself. Did you ever frighten youself because of information you received of a loved one about to make his or her transition? There is no need to perceive that as scary. Do you understand that now? You were privileged to share in the knowledge and it was a loving gesture. You may even think of it as reassuring and comforting.

Drive

You know how life can be better for humanity. You are concerned with more than just your own immediate family. You may focus on the community or even large groups of people. This is a demanding, challenging, intense energy, and no one works at this master level all the time. You are aware of something dangling in front of you that you are striving forward to obtain. This energy stimulates, encourages, prods you, keeps you moving and progressing toward your mission. You have much originality. You are a trailblazer, reformer. You may feel like mothering everyone and probably at a challenging level. If you are a teacher you may choose to teach emotionally or physically challenged children. If you have mechanical ability, you may perceive yourself an inventor.

Do be nurturing and good to yourself because this is not just a luxuriously easy life for you. You are probably leading *and* following and know when it is appropriate to do which. Adding the 1+1 together = 2. The Number 2 Chance is a resting place from intense 11 energy.

Morning Prayer

God, we thank you for the light of your joy and love touching us this morning filling us and warming our being, bringing us to full awareness of the beauty and joy in the world, enabling us to feel and see God in everything and everyone, giving us courage and strength throughout the day and allowing us to open ourselves to others so they see your love through us. Thank you God.

Chance Number 3

If you have any aspects in the following list, this Chance applies to you.

3 Life Path number
No **C, L,** or **U** in your name (lesson)
C, L, or **U** the first letter in your first name (cornerstone)
Born in **March** or **December (0-age 27)**
Born the **3rd, l2th, 21st,** or **30th** day of any month **(age 28-54)**
Born in **1902, 1911, 1920, 1929, 1938, 1947, 1956, 1965, 1974, 1983, 1992, 2001,** or **2010 (age 55-on)**

Universal Meaning

Three symbolizes "Show Biz," self-expression, self-esteem, self-image, communication skills, public relations, talent. You like to perform, like attention, the limelight, to project your personality, implant your style, like fun personalities, the joys and pleasures in life, have social potential, and use words effectively (the spoken word or the written word). You may be found on debate teams, in competitive sports, musical groups, or theater stages. You excel in something to the point of getting noticed. You may be noticed for being the best behaved, raising the biggest tomatoes, getting the best grades, having red hair, or in many other ways. A sense of humor probably sustains this "people person" when life feels a bit bumpy.

Life Path

You may want to attract fame. You may want your name to live after you're gone. You would probably be excellent in sales of any kind because of your ability with words and ability to project yourself. Whatever you do, you do it with style.

You like your life and relationships to be pleasant. You may bend over backwards to keep things pleasant and be hesitant to speak up, to say why you upset yourself, until you behave like Mount Vesuvius errupting. You have a mouth and you have a right to say whatever you want at each step so you don't accumulate stressful thoughts for weeks, months, or years and then really explode. State your opinion, but state it without expecting the other person to change. They have the right to their opinion, too.

Repressed thoughts create repressed feelings and can manifest as high blood pressure or clogged arteries. If you let your beliefs of perceived injustices eat away at you, you can create deteriorating bones or even cancer.

Birth Month Effect

(0-27 years approximately)

If you were born in March or December, something about your particular birth brought you attention. Were you premature, breech birth, overdue, a twin, first child, first grandchild, first of your sex, born in a taxi cab, first live birth to your mother? You may or may not know if there was something special, but I'm sure there was. I have never known it to be otherwise. Check with your family to find out how you were noticed. I know it is there.

Children born in March or December want attention and will usually want it from their mother (or whomever provides the primary care) in the early weeks and months. If they think they are not getting as much attention as they want because their mother is occupied with other children, working outside the home, or busy with some other activity, they will find a way to get the attention and meet their needs.

Children may become hypochondriacs because as soon as they have physical symptoms and mother is concerned, providing chicken soup, fluffing pillows, and taking their temperature, they are quick to realize, "Illness is a great way to have mother's attention."

Another way to get the needed attention is by misbehaving at school. When the child realizes the teacher's reports of poor behavior to mother means she is right there to find out what's wrong, being "naughty" becomes a wonderful tool for getting mother's attention.

The child is creative in getting attention one way or another so be sure to give this child praise, recognition, and attention for behavior and choices that you believe are appropriate, positive, and in the child's best interest.

Spiritual You

If the letter U is in your name anywhere you probably recognize the existence of an energy beyond yourself. Many people refer to this energy source as God. If the letter U is the first or second letter in your first name, you had an early experience with spiritual values. This awareness is probably a strength within you and serves you well.

Recognize Your Needs

If you are an adult with strong 3 energy, you want positive feedback, appreciation, and recognition. You are wise to recognize this in you and learn to give praise and approval to *yourself*. Satisfy your own needs with your positive self-talk every day. When you look to others for this, you are often anxious, depressed, or fearful because you *rarely* get as much attention as you think you want and *deserve*. The next step is to feel rejection, resentment, bitterness, or whatever emotion is your habit.

When you do get praise or recognition from others, the attention is like "the cherry on top of the whipped cream." Having your needs met by others is pleasant and very nice but if you make it the "Main Course," you set yourself up to feel insecure and anxious.

Learn to give yourself what you want so you free yourself to come to others out of choice, rather than need. You are the happiest when you are creative in meeting your own needs. Give yourself the hug, the pat on the back, the thank-you note, or the bouquet of flowers. Do it with love because you think good thoughts about you.

Your Goal

If you choose to meet your own needs, don't put others down because you believe they didn't meet your needs. No rational reason exists to be angry, sarcastic, or punitive to someone else. Your goal is to stop judging, labeling, and blaming and just experience and love. So let go of the belief system which keeps you unhappy because your spouse or friend doesn't remember anniversaries or special days. Take responsibility for yourself.

Your Awareness

Do you want to get to the point in your awareness that you are so loving and accepting of yourself and your right to be who you are that you will also allow the same posture for others? Awareness enables you to respond by choice to others, rather than react to others. You would no longer feel threatened by the statements, choices, opinions of others because those belong to the other person and have everything to do with them and almost nothing to do with you.

No one can make you mad, sad, or any other emotion. Your emotions are created by what you tell yourself about what the other person said. You made you mad, sad, or any other emotion. Is it rational to expect others to change what they believe, to "make you feel more comfortable?" Is it rational to reject people for being themselves?

Are you intolerant of your mother-in-law because she doesn't live by your list of "shoulds"? Release judgments of yourself and others now and free yourself and others to be who they are.

You are totally responsible for how you feel because a thought has to be thought before you feel anything. An instantaneous thought to your brain that says "This is bad for me" or "This is good for me" creates a feeling inside you. Emotions are not automatic reactions which are universally true for everyone, given the exact same circumstances. Emotions are choices you made, and because of habit they now feel automatic within you.

Both Chances 3 and 7

If Chance Number 3 and Chance Number 7 are both significant to you, it means you love people but you can only be with them so long and then you really want to be alone. You have a private, quiet side as well as a social side. Be aware of your needs and plan time for both.

Students

If you are missing C, L, and U in your name, you are here to learn all the qualities described at the beginning of this Chance. You did not come into this life with a developed self-image, or self-esteem. Until you demonstrate proficiency in this Chance and get to know and accept yourself, you could feel hollow inside when you believe you are challenged.

You have not wanted to be noticed and have been quietly in the shadows, avoiding people until this life. You may have been very shy as a child, but you get noticed for your shyness, too. An occasional tendency to round shoulders is a subconscious effort to wrap yourself around yourself and remain unnoticed.

Your higher self knows you want to experience the Number 3 Chance so you might have been a real little performer right from the beginning. Were you getting everyone's attention and performing antics that attracted noticed?

You may have utilized this energy either way, shy or outgoing. Whichever way you used it, you always attract the situations and people who are good for your ultimate progress. I am continually amazed and awed at the extent of our ability to create.

Children

Children missing C, L, and U may be helped by verbalizing to them as soon as they are born. (Even *before* the birth if you know this aspect in your child, because you have selected the name.) Verbalize to them what you are doing while you feed, bathe, change, or hold them. Use children's picture books, say the names and sounds for the animals at an early age. When they are able to speak, introduce them to friends visiting in your home and encourage them to converse when they are ready. Inviting playmates into the home for tea parties, "sleepovers," and so on encourages socialization.

Other ways to help your budding 3 Chance child includes performance-type lessons, competitive sports, clubs, debate teams, party planning, pen pals, hobbies, and playing word games.

Children are very creative in attracting their own opportunities, so parents needn't feel huge concern for being sure the children follow a set pattern. Light, friendly, loving encouragement is what I suggest.

Prayer to God

Our God, who art in heaven, hallowed be Thy name. Thy kingdom
come, Thy will be done, on Earth as it is in heaven. Give us this day our
daily bread; and forgive us our offenses as we forgive our offenders; save
us in temptation and increase our awareness for Thine is the Kingdom
and the Power and the Glory for ever. Amen.

Chance Number 4

If you have any aspects in the following list, this Chance applies to you.

4 Life Path number
13/4 Life Path number
22/4 Life Path number
No **D, M,** or **V** in your name (lesson)
D, M, or **V** the first letter in your first name (cornerstone)
Born in **April (0-age 27)**
Born the **4th, 13th, 22nd,** or **31st** day of any month **(age 28-54)**
Born in l903, **1912, 1921, 1930, 1939, 1948, 1957, 1966, 1975,
1984, 1993, 2002,** or **2011** (age 55-on)

Universal Meaning

Four symbolizes the "Rock of Gibralter." You are dependable, reliable, respectable, methodical, practical, goal oriented, organized, industrious, may be a plodder, lover of Earth who can really be counted upon. You are not afraid to work. If you give your word, I could relax knowing whatever you say you'll do will definitely be accomplished.

You probably dislike clutter but you may live with "organized clutter" because you *do* list your priorities by what's important to you. You may work where you make things take form.

You learn "short cuts" don't work because they just unravel or come undone and you are back where you started. For example, to construct a brick wall the first row of bricks is placed end to end for the entire length. It is impossible to place the second or third row of bricks until the foundation has been laid.

Life Path

You may be an efficiency expert, builder, contractor, organizer, or in any position where material things take form. Your love of Earth may inspire you to work as a horticulturist, farmer, or scientist.

Birth Month Effect

(0-27 years approximately)

If you were born in April, you may have had circumstances within your family while you were growing-up that allowed (you may feel necessitated is a better word to describe your situation) you to demonstrate your "rock" abilities. You might have needed to go to work early in your life or maybe you were the "glue" holding the family together for some reason. You might have thought something you exerienced was hard to overcome or hard to accept.

Students

If you are missing D, M, and V in your name you are here to learn all the qualities described at the beginning of this Chance. You might have been perceived as "lazy" when you were young. Or you might have been determined to confront this opportunity very early in your life and demonstrate many of the traits detailed above. You might have behaved either way because this was a new Chance for you.

Caution

If you have 4 energy from more than two or three aspects mentioned in the beginning of this Chance, you may be perceived a "workaholic," if you are into labels. (That's a joke in case you didn't recognize it.) You may be perceived as rigid and fixed in attitude and beliefs and manifest stiffness in your body. Rigid, fixed thoughts manifest as stiffness in the skeletal structure or connective tissue.

What may seem like an excess of 4 energy, certainly doesn't have to be "bad" or even "excess." It just is. You asked for that intensity for a reason. The only way surplus 4 energy is "bad" is if you are hard on yourself. You have potential for accomplishing so much with this aspect. Work with awareness because you want to, you choose to, and be good to yourself.

Children

Young children might be encouraged to practice dependability, reliability, by setting up a simple reward system for them using colorful stickers and a chart on the refrigerator. A reward system is positive reinforcement for behavior that is in their best interest.

Help children learn to keep their belongings orderly, with a place for everything, and the potential for order in their lives. A routine in the home, a study area, goal setting (short term and long term), and value in making lists are helpful.

Both Chances 4 and 5

If Chance Number 4 and Chance Number 5 are both significant to you, this combination means an interesting aspect in the outline of your life. The dependable part of you agrees to have a report on my desk at 9 A.M., tomorrow morning. You gave your word, so it *will* be there. The part of you that loves your personal freedom will impulsively accept a last-minute invitation for dinner and theater with a friend arrived in town just for the evening. You will stay awake half the night if you need to, but you will have your report on my desk in the morning. Does that feel familiar? This may be perceived as internal conflict, or stress. You probably work best under presssure.

Remember, no one is doing that to you. God isn't creating internal conflict within you, your employer isn't, your spouse, or the economy. You chose both Chances for a reason. Your awareness of the fact that you chose this aspect will help you accept the reality of how the energy manifests in your life.

Pace yourself and don't take on more projects than you can comfortably handle because there is a little kid inside of you who likes to come out and play. If you don't arrange time in your schedule for fun, you may find yourself throwing adult tantrums occasionally.

When you realize you have "done it again" to yourself, at least you can experience your projects with awareness and be good to yourself. You probably accomplish a lot and are very productive with this aspect.

Exceptional Chance

If you have any aspects in the following list, this Chance applies to you.

13/4 Life Path number
M the first letter in your first name (cornerstone)
Born the **13th** day of any month **(0-age 27)**
Born in **1903, l912, 1921, or 1930 (age 55-on)**

If this applies to you, this aspect is leadership and recognition of the highest order. You have potential to influence the emotional climate of those around you, on a team, in an office, in a family, or wherever you are. You are a "Pied Piper" in ability to attract followers and influence them. If you think positive and feel "up," your emotional outlook is felt and reflected shortly thereafter by people around you. If you are perceived negative and "down," that energy is soon felt and reflected.

Your life has the potential of rewards, fulfillment, and productivity. It could just bloom and blossom like a beautiful flower. It could be wonderful. Be aware you have a powerful aspect and maximize its potential for the benefit of yourself and others. *Always* "see your glass half full."

If you describe to me any aspect of your life as anything less than wonderful, ask yourself "What do I tell myself about this person?" (if the less than wonderful aspect is a person). Or, "What am I telling myself about this situation?" (if it's a situation). When you examine your thoughts, you realize you tell yourself perceived negative thoughts about the person or situation. Even if you told yourself "This is horrible, awful, tragic, unfair, rude and terrible," you can always find a way to change your perceived negative thoughts to positive thoughts. When you change your thoughts, you turn your life right around.

Thoughts Create

The chemistry in your body changes immediately as you change your thoughts. You can actually feel the difference because your thoughts are electrically charged and they do manifest in your body. Your body is a feedback mechanism that tells you when you experience disharmony. If you experience disharmony in your thoughts long enough, you start to take on physical symptoms and manifest dis-ease.

Nothing visually obvious actually changes when you change your thoughts, except your *perception* of the other person or situation. Your original perception resulted in your creating a down feeling in yourself. Your new perception manifests in your body a pleasant feeling.

Your Awareness

Do you choose positive or negative thoughts most often? God's gift to you is your Free Will. You can choose to think thoughts which create misery in you or thoughts which create joy. Emotional reactions by you are not automatic, either, your reactions are a choice. You learn to choose certain reactions very young, probably from a role model. They are repeated so many times they become a habit or a belief. At that point they seem automatic. Do you think there is room for some improvement in your coping skills? With increased awareness you can consciously choose to respond to outside stimuli instead of reacting in the old way. Respond instead of reacting.

What is your goal? Are you aware you are responsible for how you feel? God isn't creating your feelings, your parents aren't responsible for them, just you. Be careful what you are telling yourself because your thoughts produce the resulting feelings. Everything you experience is just that, an experience, until you judge it is good for you or bad for you. If your goal is to experience without judgment, because you have no need to upset yourself, you will observe and think and experience without reacting. Your awareness frees you to choose to respond instead of reacting.

Experience With Awareness

Nonjudgmental levels of awareness feel terrific. Would you like that? Would you like to feel free? Would you be willing to practice this idea with the weather? A temperature drop of a few degrees to the extent you feel chilled, doesn't have to mean you will "catch" cold or flu. Feeling chilled for a few minutes or a moderate amount of time can be perceived as just another experience. It isn't "bad" unless you tell yourself it is.

Feeling warmer than you usually feel while watching an outdoor event is just another experience. And so is slow traffic while driving your car or waiting in line for a service you desire.

Does anything change when you stew, fret, raise your blood pressure, boil, and tense internally? If stressing yourself made traffic move like you want it to, then it might be appropriate to do that. The truth is you have only upset yourself. Nothing else changed.

If the roof on your home blows off in a windstorm, does it put the roof back on if you cuss and swear, or sit down and cry, beat your breast, or suck your thumb in a corner? You can upset yourself over anything and everything and be miserable, if your goal is to do that. You can play "victim" or "pity poor me." The fact is the roof needs to be replaced. There is a procedure for doing that. Meanwhile, have a star-gazing party at your house, *inside*. You have the biggest skylight in town.

Daily experiences may be thought of as challenges, adventures. You can bring a sense of creativity and even a sense of humor to what you attract. What is your choice?

Another Exceptional Chance

If you have any aspects in the following list, this Chance applies to you.

22/4 Life Path number
V the first letter in your first name (cornerstone)
Born the **22nd** day of any month **(age 28-54)**
Born in **1939, 1948, 1957, 1966, 1975, 1984,** or **1993 (age 55-on)**

If this applies to you, probably you are an experienced person with a definite mission in this life. You are on the practical Earthplane but your consciousness is tapped into a much higher vibration. You are an idea person. Ideas come in you and through you that are so inspired, visionary, and idealistic. You surely are aware of this.

Do you sense things? You might label this sense intuition, imagination, perception, psychic ability, or creative talent. Do you trust your thoughts? If you pay attention to them and notice what you notice, the information will get stronger and better.

Insight

If someone told you what you sense is not logical or practical you might deny a beautiful aspect of yourself. Did you ever frighten yourself because of information you received concerning a loved one about to make their transition? There is no need to perceive that as scary. Do you understand that now? You were privileged to share in the knowledge and it was a loving gesture. You may even think of it as reassuring and comforting. Unexplained insights may occur in many aspects of your life.

Drive

You know how life can be better for humanity. You are concerned with more than just your own immediate family. You may focus on your community or large groups of people, maybe masses of people. The ideas in you raise your consciousness and they are for you to share with others.

You have chosen demanding, challenging, intense energy and no one works at that level all the time. You are like a "steamroller" in life getting up an even larger head of steam and accomplishing so much, so don't be hard on yourself. People may see you as a "workaholic" or someone who makes work out of everything. Be careful what you tell yourself. Adding the 2+2 together = 4. Chance Number 4 is a resting place from 22 energy.

Applied Idealism

You have the potential to combine vision with practical ways of making your inspired ideas take form. You are the practical idealist, a master builder of material things. You may be highly productive, fulfilled, and rewarded when accomplishing at this level. Master level energy is utilized by people who think well enough of themselves to want to give of themselves to others.

You are not motivated by desire for personal gain. You may be selfless to the point of dedication. Do be nurturing and good to yourself because this is a high energy, productive life for you.

You are an absolute survivor. It doesn't matter how you perceive "a rug has been pulled out from under you" from time to time. You are like a cat that falls out of a tree and always lands on four feet. If you perceive yourself a bit depressed, you won't stay down for long because you came to do so many wonderful things and you want to be about them. You have "worlds to conquer and mountains to climb."

The Lord is my shepherd, I shall not want. He maketh me to lie down in green pastures: he leadeth me beside the still waters. He restoreth my soul: he leadeth me in the paths of righteousness for his name's sake. Yea, though I walk through the valley of the shadow of death, I will fear no evil: for thou art with me; thy rod and thy staff they comfort me. Thou preparest a table before me in the presence of mine enemies: thou annointest my head with oil; my cup runneth over. Surely goodness and mercy shall follow me all the days of my life: and I will dwell in the house of the Lord for ever.

Psalm 23

Chance Number 5

If you have any aspects in the following list, this Chance applies to you.

5 Life Path number
No **E, N,** or **W** in your name (lesson)
Only two **Es, Ns,** or **Ws** (lesson)
E, N, or **W** the first letter in your first name (cornerstone)
Born in **May (0-age 27)**
Born the **5th, 14th,** or **23rd** day of any month **(age 28-54)**
Born in **1904, 1913, 1922, 1931, 1940, 1949, 1958, 1967, 1976, 1985, 1994,** 2003, or 2012 (age 55-on)

Universal Meaning

Five symbolizes experiences of the five senses, an active participant in life. You want to experience life for yourself in order to learn from it. You scatter your energy, are "Jack of all trades and master of none." You love travel, adventure, personal freedom, variety, and choices. You are a juggler who keeps all the balls bouncing. You are willing to risk in daily living activities because you learn so much that way. You develop good common sense when you risk a bit to try new things.

You are flexible, adaptable, willing to go with the flow, expect the unexpected, and never bored because you are a busy, mainstream person. Several house moves, a different routine or set of circumstances to confront at work each day, impulsiveness, all are possibilities for your curious Chance Number 5. This is the Chance of your humanness, your physical appetite, your zest for life.

Because of your impulsive nature, "That sounds like fun, let's try it, let's do it," you may perceive you are in "hot water" occasionally. A learning situation is always inherent in what you perceive a mistake. You don't learn by your successes. You learn by what you perceive as mistakes so don't be so hard on yourself. It's O.K. That's how you learn.

Life Path

You may be a travel agent, writer, performer, merchant seaman, soldier of fortune, public official, professional courier, or in any area in which you have variety and personal freedom.

Birth Month Effect

(0-27 years approximately)

If you were born in May you might have moved one or more times, traveled extensively, and run your mother a merry chase wondering which direction you went in last because you were an active child. You scatter your energy and stay busy every minute. You want to experience life for yourself in order to learn. Your freedom is important to you.

Children

Young children are usually active, adventurous. They want to try everything and are sometimes labeled "daredevils." Girls often pick up the label "tomboy." They may be the first one to the top of the oak tree, the first one to swim to the raft or the first one to figure out how to jump safely off the roof of the garage.

Adults

Adults are young at heart and will always have a youthful curiosity about life. I can't imagine you ever old in body, mind, or spirit because you enjoy so many interests. You may register for special interest classes or take up a new sport at an advanced age. No rocking chair for you. If you had one you probably would be arrested for speeding in it.

If you have children or grandchildren they probably think you are a fun, "with it" person. A little kid inside you wants to come out and play. So be sure to schedule time for fun in your busy schedule.

If you go shopping for a new red coat you won't buy the first red coat you see. You probably go into every store in the mall before you make a decision because you love choices. That's the only reason you want money. It gives you the choices so important to you. Without money you have few choices.

Caution

If you have an abundance of Es, Ns, and Ws, you may think to settle down in one location for any length of time is difficult. You may want to make changes for the sake of change. You may manifest this Chance in another way also. If you have *many* fives, you may have been so active in the past you just rest and stay put this time. You have Free Will, so how you utilize the energy is your choice.

Students

Most people have three or more of any combination of E, N, or W in their name. For those letters to be missing is unusual. If you are missing E, N, and W in your name you are here to learn all the qualities described at the beginning of this Chance. You came into this life with a lack of experience in day to day living. You may be fairly fixed, regimented, and rigid in your outlook. You have little flexibility, adaptability, and may really be distressed at changes in routine, schedule, or geographic location of your family.

You want to develop common sense from daily living experiences. You may be overly cautious, dislike crowds, and as a child be unwilling to confront this Chance. You may want to cling to your old ways for a while. The energy may be used either way with any of the Chances. Relax, it's O.K. "It will all come out in the wash." Your subconscious knowledge of this Chance to be learned motivates you to attract opportunities to experience it.

Parent Awareness

If your child is learning and demonstrating this Chance, you can understand your child's adventures if you are assured all experiences are part of their divine unfolding, all for their ultimate growth and development. You relate to your child in a more harmonious way when you know where experience is being acquired and encourage growth in that specific area. Your child may have a short attention span when he or she is little, so be patient. Encourage your child to try new things and risk a bit, within reason.

This Chance can seem a bit scary to parents, if you fear your child may make "mistakes." You have every right to guide your child confidently in ways comfortable to you. You have a right to peace of mind. I am not suggesting parents abdicate their guidance role, just a balance and an awareness of why the child does what he or she does. Also, the awareness to know we do learn more by our "mistakes" than from our successes. Our perceived mistakes are stressful, or even emotionally painful, or physically painful, and we are motivated to evaluate, stretch ourselves a bit, and find a better way the next time.

Successes are pleasant. Why would success motivate a person to change or grow? The thought "If it isn't broken don't fix it" is what you may tell yourself at some level of your consciousness.

Both Chances 5 and 4

(See page 69.)

Both Chances 5 and 7

If you are demonstrating Chance Number 5 and Chance Number 7, this is really a helpful balance. You probably don't do anything you perceive as really extreme, wild, or crazy because you always have a little voice inside you saying, "Wait, wait a minute. You better think your idea through because you may not be delighted with the outcome of this choice."

Parents can relax their anxious thoughts about their child's choices if the child has this balance. The child probably will make reasonable choices. You have no need to feel anxious anyway, but you have even less perceived reason with this aspect.

Chance Number 6

If you have any aspects in the following list, this Chance applies to you.

6 *Life Path number*
33/6 *Life Path number*
No **F, O,** or **X** in your name (lesson)
F, O, or **X** the first letter in your first name (cornerstone)
Born in **June (0-age 27)**
Born the **6th, 15th,** or **24th** day of any month **(age 28-54)**
Born in l905, l914, l923, 1932, 1941, l950, l959, 1968, 1977, 1986, 1995, 2004, or 2013 **(age 55-on)**

Universal Meaning

Six symbolizes family, the domestic scene, responsibility assumed willingly within the family, office, on a team, committee, even an extended family. You commit to finish what you start, you love peace and harmony around you, hate to have any one mad at you and are willing to make small adjustments within yourself to maintain peace and harmony around you.

Life Path

People experiencing the Chance Number 6 want to balance, compromise, mediate. You may be a doctor, lawyer, teacher, interior designer, dietitian, exterior designer, home builder, any work connected to the family unit or the domestic scene. You may be in a fatherly or parental role in whatever you do. You probably enjoy a position in which people come to you with a situation they want resolved, and you offer them expertise.

Family is so important to you. You may be the center of an adoring family. Are you the one who invites everyone to your house on special holidays? Are you the person who plans the family reunions? Keeps the family album?

Birth Month Effect

(0-27 years approximately)

If you were born in June, you may have made a lot of adjustments within yourself because of something going on in the family in which you lived. It might have been an elderly person in your home, a divorce or separation, a physically or mentally handicapped person, an adoption, foster children, the long absence of one parent for various reasons, substance abuse, or many other situations. These are all opportunities to learn the dynamics of family life and willingly assume responsibility.

Students

If you are missing F, O, and X in your name, you are here to learn all the qualities described at the beginning of this Chance. If you don't fully understand the give and take within a family, or if you are unaware or unwilling to make adjustments within yourself you may separate or divorce. Learning this Chance certainly doesn't have to work that way. That is just one way it may work. If you experience divorce, it is a learning situation and not the end of the world. If you didn't learn the lesson you attracted, you may attract a similar situation. Use common sense and keep communicating to resolve differences to the best of your ability. If you just walk away from a perceived problem in your marriage, you may have overlooked your Chance and be facing it again in a different disguise.

Willing Responsibility

Whatever responsibility you agree to accept, do it because you want to, you choose to. Do the responsibility with love or don't do it. When you agree to take on responsibility because you believe "A good friend should help out a friend" or "A good son, brother, wife, or parent should do this," you bring resentment and bitterness to whatever you agree to do. Your negative thoughts manifest and you sabotage yourself.

If you make a bed out of duty instead of choice, you may hit your shin on the corner of the bed, pull something in your back bending over to smooth the covers, or jam a fingernail tucking the sheets under the mattress.

Insight

The next time you agree to accept a responsibility and the project isn't going well, examine your thoughts and motives. If the project is something you are definitely going to do, why not make the best of it by "choosing" to do it and let the energy flow unimpeded? You can make a project difficult for yourself if you choose to by feeling unhappy, frustrated, and miserable while assuming the responsibility to which you agreed. Some people continue to live their entire life from a victim position. Feeling like a victim creates a habit. With awareness, you can change your thoughts and live your life with joy.

Your Rights

You have a mouth and if you don't want to do something you were asked to do, saying "No" is much better for you and certainly more honest. Can you say "No" to a family member without feeling guilty? Do you feel compelled to do most of the things others ask you to do?

If I ask you to iron my blouse because I'm in a big hurry and I need to leave in five minutes, what would you say? If you say "Oh, sure," but you really don't want to iron my blouse, you may burn your finger on the iron or scorch my blouse. Then you have to remove the scorch *and* iron my blouse. You may iron into a button on the front closing when you get around to that part, and the button falls off. Then you feel obligated to sew the button back on in addition to ironing the blouse. Could you say "No" to me, or "Wear a different blouse," or "I don't want to iron your blouse" without feeling guilty? You have the right to speak for yourself.

Special Awareness

You really don't help me (in an emergency *yes,* but not in the long run) by ironing the blouse anyway because you enable me in postponing the very Chance I want to learn. I attracted this "stressful" situation because I want to learn to plan ahead, be better organized, or more responsible for myself. The very things that burden me and perplex me are those exact things I attract for my growth. If this is a very rare request and you want to iron the blouse, fine. Please do it with love or don't do it.

Your Aura

Another part of this Chance has to do with an aura (energy field) about you that attracts friends, relatives, even strangers telling you their "problems." They see you as a wise counselor.

Your willingness to listen to others is a wonderful gift of yourself. You are doing a lot by being there for other people. You don't have to solve their "problem" for them, or "rescue" them from their perceived dilemma. They are perfectly capable of resolving the situation themselves. They attracted the "problem" for a reason. Practice hearing yourself saying something like "You really are having a hard time with this. What are you going to do?" Do you hear what happens? You throw the ball back to them.

You demean the other person in your mind by thinking he or she isn't capable of figuring it out and you *are* capable. You may want to offer suggestions. If you have expertise in a professional capacity you will certainly offer helpful information. There is no need to make the perceived problem *your* problem.

Thoughts Create

If you are inclined to take on others' "problems" and think of them as yours, and you take on the problems vividly and dramatically presented in living color on the 6 P.M. and 11 P.M. television news, you may actually develop back problems. The weight of the world gets very heavy to carry around on your shoulders.

Listen all you want. Your willingness to listen is a love gift you offer to others. Release yourself from assuming their responsibilities though, because that is an opportunity for them to learn and that's why they're here.

Children

Children missing F, O, and X in their name can be encouraged to learn this Chance by suggesting two or three household responsibilities within their capability and allowing them to select one or two they agree to do on a regular basis. The responsibilities can be rotated or rethought every week or so, depending on the child's age. A chart on the wall and attractive stickers which your child places on the chart as the responsibility is completed would serve as motivation for a while. Another way for children to learn about responsibility is by caring for a pet of their own. This method needs supervision until you feel confident your child provides proper care of the pet.

Keep in mind this Chance has to do with assuming responsibility willingly. Children are to learn to do this because they want to, they choose to. Doing it out of duty or shoulds defeats the Chance. Be patient with them.

Caution

If you have more than two or three aspects in the list of Chance Number 6, you may be overly serious about being responsible, almost duty bound. You are a person who may think you "Keep your nose to the grindstone." You may be hard on yourself and those around you because you are so conscientious. You may try to parent everyone.

Exceptional Chance

If you have the aspect below, this Chance applies to you.

33/6 *Life Path number*

If this applies to you, probably you are an experienced person with a definite mission in this life. You are on the practical Earthplane but your consciousness is tapped into a much higher vibration. You are an idea person. Ideas come in you and through you which are so inspired, visionary, and idealistic. You surely are aware of this. Do you sense things? You might label this sense intuition, a big imagination, perceptive, psychic ability, good at pretending, or a creative talent. Do you trust your thoughts? If you pay attention to them and notice what you notice, the information will grow stronger and better.

Insight

If someone told you that what you sense is not logical or practical, you might deny a beautiful aspect of yourself. Did you ever frighten yourself because of information you received of a loved one about to make their transition? There is no need to perceive that as scary. Do you understand that now? You were privileged to share in the knowledge. The information was a loving gesture. You may even think of it as reassuring and comforting. Seemingly unexplained insights may occur in many aspects of your life.

Drive

You know how life can be better for humanity. Family is extremely important to you and usually weighs heavily upon you. You are concerned with more than your own immediate family. You may focus on your community, or large groups of people, maybe masses of people. You are like a cosmic parent parenting everyone. The ideas in you raise your consciousness. And they are for you to demonstrate by example in *your* life, in order to inspire others.

You have chosen a demanding, challenging, intense energy and no one works at this master level all the time. Adding the 3+3 together = 6. The Chance Number 6 is a resting place from 33 energy.

Selfless Service

You have the potential to combine vision with the practical knowledge of how to apply it and the selflessness to serve humanity to a point that goes beyond assuming responsibility willingly to the point of dedication or possibly sacrifice. This energy is the highest form of service on the Earthplane. You have the potential for bringing Light to humanity. You may be highly productive, fulfilled, and inwardly rewarded when accomplishing at this level. Master level energy is utilized by people who think well enough of themselves to want to give themselves to others. Be nurturing and good to yourself because this is a very special life for you.

You came to accomplish so much. Your personal drive to serve humanity could feel like an obsession. So keep the awareness of just living each present moment. You are determined to shed Light in the world and you will — you are already shedding Light now. Do it one step at a time. You are an absolute survivor. It doesn't matter how you perceive a rug was pulled out from under you, occasionally. You are like a cat who falls out of a tree and always lands on four feet. Best wishes to you on your life of service.

Jesus was a 33/6.

Chance Number 7

If you have any aspects in the following list, this Chance applies to you.

7 Life Path number
No **G, P,** or **Y** in your name (lesson)
G, P, or **Y** the first letter in your first name (cornerstone)
Born in **July (0-age 27)**
Born the **7th, l6th,** or **25th** day of any month **(age 28-54)**
Born in **1906, 1915, 1924, 1933, 1942, 1951, 1960, 1969, 1978,**
1987, 1996, 2005, or 2014 (age 55-on)

Universal Meaning

Seven symbolizes the inner spiritual number, a spectator and observer of life, a private person. Sometimes you like to be by yourself. You can be alone and not lonely. Your hobby or interest like reading, writing, research into genealogy, chemistry experiments, or bird watching seems to necessitate your being by yourself, isolating yourself. The reverse is actually true. Your desire to be alone motivated you to develop hobbies and interests so you have a good reason for being by yourself.

You may think you are a loner, different, or aloof. You have a wonderful mind capable of abstract, complicated, technical things. You are cautious and reserved in certain areas of your life. You understand the benefit of transfering fears into faith.

Life Path

You probably prefer long robes or gowns. Perhaps you enjoy a graduation-type robe or choir robe. Subconsciously, you believe yourself to be like a high priest or priestess because you have enormous ancient wisdom within you.

You know things you have no way of knowing from experiences in this life exclusively. You didn't experience the knowledge for yourself, no one told you, and you didn't read about it. Still you know.

You probably are in something involved with spiritual or mental activity. You usually are the brains, or the inspiration behind whatever you do. You may be a scientist, writer, researcher, journalist, historian, minister, missionary, computer programmer, watch repair person or in any other mental discipline.

You can do complicated, technical things, and you love to analyze and think things through. You may have a tendency to overanalyze an opportunity until it passes you by.

Birth Month Effect

(0-27 years approximately)

If you were born in July, you might have had a difficult time during early childhood, elementary school years, or junior high because you felt different from the other children at a time when most children want to be just like everyone else. You might have created a negative image of yourself and developed insecurities which need to be released and changed so you can go forward effectively.

Children strongly demonstrating the Chance Number 7 may choose to spend hours in their room alone, listening to music, reading, writing, or on a computer. They may want to spend long hours observing nature, walking a beach, or floating on a raft in front of their cottage. Don't frustrate them by insisting they go out and play with someone. Avoid labeling these children and just accept and love them. They are who they are.

If you are uncomfortable around this type of child, that is an opportunity for you to learn and grow. There is no need for you to perceive something is "wrong" with the child.

Students

If you are missing G, P, and Y in your name, you are here to learn all the qualities described at the beginning of this Chance. The vast majority of people alive on Earth now came to experience this. Hundreds of years ago, to be a spiritual person often meant isolation, deprivation, maybe even flagellation and hair shirts. The average person didn't want any part of that because it looked like a terrible way to live life.

You don't have to make extreme sacrifices now to learn to be a spiritual person. The fact that almost everyone is paying attention to experiencing this Chance tells me a wonderful spiritual awakening is taking place on our planet. Our consciousness is being raised. We are getting better and better.

The fact that we are so horrified with certain world news is because we know the world doesn't have to be that way. We know there is a better way of handling people and situations. That is why we are so appalled when certain events occur.

Children

Children missing these letters in their name can be encouraged to learn this Chance by teaching them to calm and center themselves, to meditate, or pray. There are many ways to learn and you are creatively drawn to be at the right place, at the right time to experience whatever is in your best interest. You might have a pet die when you are a young person, and you might have been mad at it for dying and leaving you. You might have been mad at God because you thought God took your pet. That type of experience can certainly help to start you thinking, asking, searching for answers to spiritual questions. Losing a friend or loved one when you are young or at any age is another way.

Both Chances 7 and 5

(See page 78.)

Both Chances 7 and 3

(See page 64.)

Spiritual You

If you have any two of the letters G, P, or Y in your entire name, such as **Phyllis, Gary, George, Gregory, Stephany,** and so on, you probably were a very highly placed spiritual person such as a priest, nun, or monk in a previous incarnation. (Include your middle name and last name to determine this aspect.)

You may or may not have religious affiliation in this life. The existence of beautiful spiritual values within you is not to be confused with church attendance in an organized religion. The organized religions have fear attached to them to control their worshippers. I don't believe fear has anything to do with God. God's nature is pure love. God isn't waiting to punish us when we "die."

We are God's child and God doesn't just love good children. God loves all children. You may still be strongly involved with religious institutions, but not necessarily. This aspect can go either way. You are very comfortable being alone. In fact, you want some private time for yourself each day if you can arrange it.

Insight to Aloneness

The belief that people living alone are "so lonely" is a myth. It doesn't have to follow that people who live alone are automatically lonely. That idea is often propounded regarding senior citizens.

Loneliness is a feeling which comes from within. It starts with a thought first and then the feeling manifests. The thought always has to come first. That's how you program your computer brain which does not question but just obeys. You might feel lonely in a crowd or in a large family because of what you're telling yourself. Be aware of your thoughts.

Caution

If you have Chance Number 7 from several aspects, you may perceive an excess of this energy. It is there by choice and it is there for a reason. An abundance of 7 energy doesn't have to be "bad" or an "imbalance." You may have a tendency to go within to the extent that activities and choices can border on escaping. People sometimes choose to escape into sleep, food, work, sports, even abuse of drugs or alcohol.

You probably are conditioned (programmed) to think escaping is absolutely "bad" because it may mask learning situations and hinder opportunity to progress. Escaping into drugs for example certainly isn't a way I choose to experience my lessons but to learn through the perceived pain of one's excesses is also possible. If you really understand yourself and are consciously aware of the potential of this Chance you can be creative and channel perceived excesses in ways that are in your best interest.

Transfer Fears

Sometimes people misuse the caution or analytical aspect of this Chance until they know better. They may describe themselves as a worrier or fretter. Is that you? Do you stew and fret over loved ones' safety? Are you afraid for your friends and family to fly in airplanes? Do you worry about your child crossing streets or taking drivers' training? Do you notice a few more gray hairs or new wrinkles around your eyes? Worrying is a habit and can be demonstrated over frivolous things and even more substantial things.

Ultimate Fear

I suppose the ultimate worry is that loved ones or friends may die. I don't believe dying is the absolute worst thing happening to a wonderful human being. Dying is just shedding your body which isn't you anyway. Dying is just releasing your physical form as you retain your spiritual form. I think of dying as a revolving door because very little actually happens.

Everything in existence is matter and to destroy anything is impossible. Matter can only change from one form to another. That fabulous energy which is you is always just as intact as it ever was. So if you release yourself from the fear of people dying, you free yourself to experience your life to the fullest.

Negative Attraction

To feel bad, fret, or worry does not help anyone. In fact, it may impact in an undesirable way because of your negative imagery. One universal law states: *"We attract what we fear the most."* I'm sure you don't want to do that.

Release Fear

Worry is usually about something in the future and it almost never happens. Worry is a drain of energy. I used to stew and mull over a "worry" until I was aware of my seeming inability to resolve it. I couldn't resolve the worry because it was something in the future and it hadn't happened yet, or it really wasn't "my problem" to solve anyway. I would let go of one worry and go on to the next "worry," going from one to another in my head. I thought of them like the luggage at an airport going around and around on a conveyor belt until someone removes it.

The Green Book

Do you see yourself in the picture I am describing? Do yourself a favor and get a bright green notebook. One for something around a dollar would be just fine. I favor green, because it is the color of abundance. Abundance in health, wealth, happiness, or any other condition. Whenever you are aware of worrying about anything, write it in your green book. Put flight numbers, arrival and departure times, airline, and destinations in your green book.

If you read children were burned over 40 percent of their bodies in a house fire and you concern yourself for their recovery, put them in your green book. Put local and national elections in your book, if you concern yourself about political issues. Anything at all you find yourself noticing with concern, put all concerns in your green book.

Then, anytime you pray, meditate, or any time you think of the green book say:

> *Dear God, thank you for the release of all the concerns in the green book to the Light. And this is so.*

When you release concerns to the highest power of the universe, God, you have no need to continue carrying those thoughts around inside of you. Releasing your concerns, frees you to put your energy into other areas. You do something entirely constructive instead of just worrying.

Insight to Prayer

If you pray, be very careful what you ask for because you are likely to receive it. Your words create because they are electrically charged. Pray as though your prayers are already accomplished because that demonstrates ultimate faith.

Are you aware you could evoke prayer and healing whenever you are in a large gathering of people, public places, sporting events, anywhere, without ever saying a word aloud? You can really help yourself and humanity by being aware of this opportunity. Enormous energy is concentrated in one place when people are in a theater, church, concert hall, or stadium. This energy may be evoked, gathered, and utilized for the benefit of the entire Earth.

Get Ready

Take a few long, slow, deep breaths in through your nose. Hold the air a few seconds, then slowly exhale fully and deeply through slightly parted lips.

Words said within your body such as:

Thank you for the love and Light surrounding, enfolding, and protecting everyone and everything in this airplane, (wherever you are). Thank you for the release of Light from the Light center in every person to expand and fill every cell in their body with healing energy and to permeate throughout their body, mind, and spirit. Thank you for their perfect health, their affluence, their thoughts of being loved, their healthy ego, and for the awakening of the Christ Consciousness within them to radiate further throughout the planet earth and beyond. And this is so.

When you hear sirens from emergency vehicles, you are compassionately helpful to think:

Thank you for White Light surrounding the cause of this concern. And this is so.

You do something positive to help with this awareness. You are a kind of "jumper cable" to people or a situation in stress or deficit.

Thought Forms Heal

The thoughts you think can accurately be perceived as prayers. Prayers are more consciously organized perhaps, but your very thought can heal another person. For example, think of a person who has a broken arm. The best way for you to picture him or her is whole, healthy, in perfect condition, functioning 100 percent. Your visual imagery of people in total health and harmony with their environment energizes in a positive way to promote healing. Thinking of them as a "little bird with a broken wing" is energizing negatively and helps to keep the status quo. Your thoughts are electrically charged, they manifest, they create.

Insight to Healing

Other aspects play a big part in healing. "Sickness" serves two purposes. It gets you something you didn't know how to get otherwise, like attention, love, a vacation, rest, chicken soup from a friend, or other things. Or "sickness" gets you out of something you didn't know how to get out of otherwise like being responsible for yourself, caring for an elderly parent, going some place you didn't want to go, doing your own vacuuming, or for other reasons of your own.

If the elimination of every disease and every physical symptom were possible in the next five minutes, we would just create new ones because they serve us so well.

When you initiate a lawsuit for personal injury and suffering, a direct relationship exists between the length of the litigation and the degree of pain and suffering you perceive. You heal much faster when you do not need to blame someone else for what you attracted.

Chance Number 8

If you have any aspects in the followng list, this Chance applies to you.

8 *Life Path number*
No **H, Q,** or **Z** in your name (lesson)
H, Q, or **Z** the first letter in your first name (cornerstone)
Born in **August (0-age 27)**
Born the **8th, 17th,** or **26th** day of **any month (age 28-54)**
Born in **1907, 1916, 1925, 1934, 1943, 1952, 1961, 1970, 1979,**
1988, 1997, 2006, or **2015 (age 55-on)**

Universal Meaning

Eight symbolizes money, material possessions, showing a profit, upward mobility financially, executive ability, success, achievement, recognition, wielding power, and administrating. You see commercial ventures in daily living and your security is important to you. If I were to give you a gift, I wouldn't give you some little, cheap item, because you appreciate beautiful things.

There are varying degrees of wielding power, so you don't have to occupy the White House or be president of General Motors to wield power. If you are a mother who keeps family members' schedules for lessons, the orthodontist, scout meetings, and still has clean socks and underwear available most of the time, you are demonstrating Chance Number 8.

Life Path

You are often in positions of authority, positions of power, executives, managers, directors. You are the movers and shakers, the supervisors, organizers. You mastermind events and know how to accomplish commercial ventures.

Birth Month Effect

(0-27 years approximately)

If you were born in August, you may have had some difficulty handling this Chance. You may have had a rather frustrating childhood because this energy involves wielding power, showing a profit, executive ability, and similar methods of wielding power. What little child has an opportunity to do that? About all you can do is have a lemonade stand, put on shows in your backyard and sell tickets, be treasurer of your cub scout pack, or involve yourself in student government in junior high, or high school. Possibly what you did was decide to live better materially as an adult than you did as a child. Is that how it worked for you? A child cannot work with this energy easily.

You might have postponed this Chance from your childhood phase (0-27 years) to a later time and confronted your birthday phase (28-54 years) for your first phase. You know how you are experiencing this Chance. Read both Chances and decide how that fits for you.

Students

If you are missing H, Q, and Z in your name, you are here to learn all the qualities described at the beginning of this Chance. You did not come into this life with good judgment regarding money matters and that is something you want to learn.

You might have chosen to be born into a very affluent family and then let money slip through your fingers and feel the loss of it. You might have spent your entire inheritance, have nothing to show for the money, and be back to square one to learn how to handle money. You learn out of your perceived pain because you believe there must be a better way and you stretch yourself and grow.

You might have been born into an affluent family and thought money was a burden because you felt inadequate in knowing how to invest and manage money in any competent manner.

You might have felt overwhelmed by what you thought was needed in financial expertise to maintain and sustain your lifestyle. You might have felt embarrassed by your family's wealth, ashamed to invite your friends to your home because of your perceived view of excessive ostentation. This can work many ways.

You might have experienced this Chance by being born into a less than affluent family and you wondered how anyone ever accumulated enough money to afford the wonderful material things you wanted. You probably appreciate lovely things and want to learn this Chance because of the possible deprivation of your early years. The contrast of your lifestyle to what you noticed around you might have motivated you to learn the money Chance.

Thoughts Manifest

You may think you have no perceived problem with handling money at all. You may really hang onto money and squirrel it away for a rainy day. Do you see yourself as thrifty and a saver? That method is not handling money. Holding on to money is hoarding it. If you pinch pennies and hang onto your money you are probably experiencing the symptoms of constipation. It's true. Your thoughts manifest in your body. That's the way your body functions as a feedback machine.

When you write checks to pay utilities, taxes, charge accounts, or any bills just bless the transaction and send it along. You are going to pay your bills, right? It is in your best interest to learn to pay them with love. You can pay them willingly, begrudgingly, bitterly, happily, or in several other negative ways. Why not pay them with love? You receive something in exchange for the energy called money. Your thoughts create. A law of physics states: *A vacuum must first be created in order for it to be filled.* Visualize yourself releasing money to make room for more money. Practice it.

Caution

You may want to consult a financial advisor when you make a purchase of some consequence such as stocks, real estate, home improvement, automobile, or any large investment. You are new in this arena so be sure to ask lots of questions of an attorney, financial consultant, or investment banker because you cannot abandon your opportunity to learn. Do not assume these professionals *always* have your best interest at heart.

Insight

This Chance could be feast or famine depending on what you tell yourself. What do you think you deserve? You are God's child. You deserve the best. Do you think if others already acquired a lot of money, you won't be able to *have* a lot of money because there is a limit to the money available? There is enough in this beautiful world for every one of us to have everything in abundance if we just have the awareness to allow it. Open your awareness to the possibilities and enjoy.

Do you think you aren't worthy? That money has to come "hard"? Or you should "labor" for money? Do you believe money is something "evil"? Do you believe people with money are often unhappy, or miserable? I know people who are miserable, with or without money.

If you wait to be happy until you win the lottery, I doubt that will create the happiness. You are as happy as you make up your mind to be, with or without winning the lottery. Happiness is an attitude, an outlook, and has nothing to do with money.

As far as I can tell, the only thing money does for you is give you choices. Without money, you don't have many choices. Money certainly does not guarantee health or happiness. It only gives you choices.

Irrational Thoughts

You may want to have money working for you and get on a perceived gravy train as someone you know seems to have done. If you think because someone is part of an affluent family they know about handling money, you may set yourself up for some real disappointments. That is an irrational perception. Resist the temptation to make assumptions about other people based on appearances, life style, what others say about them or any other source.

For example, if you have a friend whom you perceive is moving upward materially, you might decide your friend is working with Number 8 Chance and conclude all kinds of things because of your belief. You may want to invest money with this person because you believe him or her to be a good business partner. By the time you realize your friend is motivated by wanting to be noticed, wanting attention, or recognition (Chance Number 3) the financial venture might look like a roller coaster ride.

Erroneous Conclusions

People in perceived positions of power may be there because of Chance Number 8 but it could also be from Chance Number 3 as I just described, or even Chance Number 5. If personal freedom, variety, and choices are important to you, you may pay attention to financial dealings to afford your love of choices. Reality is not always as it seems.

Do be careful about drawing conclusions with any Chance because drawing erroneous conclusions is very easy even when you see something with your own eyes or hear something with your own ears. It happens all the time and sometimes you don't know that you don't know and you go on your ignorant way. That is really worth repeating. Sometimes, you don't know that you don't know.

The following story illustrates this point and influences my daily outlook enormously. I believe it may help you also.

The Frog

A scientist decided to conduct an experiment to determine what happens under certain conditions with a frog trained to jump on command.

To conduct the experiment, the scientist first removed the right, front foot of the frog. He gave the command "Jump, frog, jump!" and the frog jumped. He wrote in his scientific journal, "When the right, front foot of the frog is removed, it still jumps."

Next he removed the left, front foot of the frog and repeated "Jump, frog, jump!" It jumped. He noted in his journal, "the frog still jumped."

He removed the back, right foot of the frog and it still jumped. He noted that as he had the other times. He removed the fourth foot of the frog and gave the usual command. The frog didn't move. He gave the command again, "Jump frog, jump!" Nothing happened.

He repeated the command once more, but there was no movement by the frog. The scientist recorded in his journal: "When the fourth foot of the frog is removed, the frog loses its hearing."

An erroneous conclusion is so easy to draw. Be aware of this possibility in your life and remember the simple story. You will find situations in your life every day where you can utilize the message it carries.

Children

Children missing H, Q, and Z could be helped by giving them an allowance when they are about six or seven years old and insisting they budget it. A budget is not a punishment, it is a spending plan. The word budget sounds restrictive but if you call it a spending plan you are more likely to stick with it. You have a set amount of money and specific needs. A spending plan helps to balance the two. Handling money is not a monumental task unless you make it so. Your child would have some money to spend, some to save, possibly some for Sunday school or other categories.

If your child wants to go to the store with a friend to buy something but doesn't have any money, give him/her a big hug and say, "Honey, on Tuesday you will receive your allowance again, and you will have a chance to decide again how you want to spend your money." Another option would be to suggest earning additional money by cleaning bathroom sinks, emptying wastebaskets, or other appropriate jobs. Don't "bail them out." If you freely give children money, you are an enabler who is helping them postpone the lesson they have attracted. They will need to be more and more creative in attracting situations where they learn to handle money as an energy.

If you are a woman who was "bailed out" by your parents and later by a husband, you may have a real struggle confronting and learning the Chance Number 8 for yourself. Your support system actually aids you in prolonging and postponing your opportunities to learn.

Chance Number 9

If you have any aspects in the following list, this Chance applies to you.

9 Life Path number
No **I** or **R** in your name (lesson)
Only one **I** or **R** (lesson)
I or **R** the first letter in your first name (cornerstone)
Born in **September (0-age 27)**
Born the **9th, 18th,** or **27th** day of any month **(age 28-54)**
Born in **1908, 1917, 1926, 1935, 1944, 1953, 1962, 1971, 1980, 1989, 1998, 2007,** or **2016 (age 55-on)**

Universal Meaning

Nine symbolizes the universal brotherhood of man, tolerance, compassion, forgiveness, love, generosity, emotions, sentiment, compatibility, selflessness, giving of oneself.

You experienced enough pain, or emotion in your life that when you are around someone who is hurting, you recognize their emotion and want to reach out to them. You might say "Are you alright?" or "Is something bothering you?" You understand and recognize feelings, emotions in yourself and others. You feel things deeply. You would feel miserable if you couldn't give of yourself because you love to be of service to others. At some level of your consciousness you know we are all brothers and sisters. You recognize the oneness connecting us all.

Life Path

Occupations may include any type of service to others, philanthropic opportunities, the arts, social work, and even travel agents because this Chance often deals with long distance travel or world travel.

Birth Month Effect

(0-27 years approximately)

If you were born in September, this Chance almost always involves completion. You may come into situations at the exact moment to "tie the ribbon around and put the bow on top." You finish, complete, bring to a conclusion many things. You experience many changes within yourself, a personal "house cleaning."

Most Compatible

Nine is a fascinating number because it is the only number you can add to any other single number and when the two numbers are added together, the result is.always the single number again.

Example: 9+4=13

1+3=4

Example: 9+6=15

1+5=6

A similar situation occurs when nine is multiplied by any other single number. In this situation the result is always the nine again.

Example: 9x2=18

1+8=9

Example: 9x5=45

                  4+5=9

Nine is the only number which has this trait. This means you are usually compatible with everyone. You probably get along very well with people and you are at home wherever you find yourself. You are just as comfortable talking to people at an inner city mission as meeting people at a posh club. You understand we are all brothers and sisters; and you understand God will be just as pleased to see the wino who has often passed out in the gutter come through the "revolving door" as God will be to see any one of us. We are all God's children. There is only God, and we are all "chips off the old block" if you care to think of our relationship with God that way.

Law of Giving

This Chance Number 9 is working with the universal law of giving. Simply stated: *Whatever you give to others comes back to you tenfold.* If you give out love, compassion, tolerance, and forgiveness, that comes back to you tenfold. If you give out prejudice, intolerance, bigotry, and hatred, that comes back tenfold. The law of giving is a universal law which cannot be altered or ignored.

Spirit of Giving

If you give a gift and then anticipate a thank-you note, that transaction is not the true spirit of giving. When you believe a gift "should" be followed by a thank-you note that is actually an exchange.

The true spirit of giving is to give because you want to give, and with no thought of return. If you want a note stating "Thank you so much for the beautiful gift. You were so wonderful to think of me. You are a thoughtful, generous person. You are my favorite relative and I love you so much," and so on, you are giving a gift to encourage the person to think you're wonderful. The note helps to inflate your perceived inadequate self-esteem.

When you receive a note, it is "the old cherry again" (you know, the one on top of the whipped cream). A note is very pleasant but if you make it the "Main Course" you are not giving in the true spirit of giving. Further, you upset and frustrate yourself when you anticipate a note which may or may not be forthcoming. Your expectation that you "should" receive a note sets you up to feel angry, disappointed, or whatever emotion you choose to feel when there is no note.

You have every right to verify that the gift arrived if you wonder whether it arrived or not. To tell yourself the recipient was thoughtless, unappreciative, or rude because you didn't receive a note is irrational and such a drain of your energy. You are "leap frogging" with that assumption. (See page 97, "The Frog.")

Give because you want to, you choose to. Bless the gift and send it along, no strings attached. You will feel a beautiful freedom within you when you let go of the old belief system requiring an exchange instead of giving a gift.

Good manners and etiquette may dictate a note but we each have our own list of "shoulds" and some people grew up in families where that idea was never practiced. You have no control over other people's behavior. To upset yourself about something over which you have no control is a waste of energy. You certainly can upset yourself if you want to, but why do you want to? Let go of old beliefs now.

Metamorphosis

You are slowly changing, emerging, evolving, blooming, and blossoming like a beautiful flower. Your consciousness is raising. You are like the caterpillar worm which spins a cocoon and emerges as a beautiful moth. The message isn't that the worm is "bad" and the moth is "good." Both are wonderful. The message is that you emerge wiser and different than before. You may look back on your life over ten or fifteen years and think you can hardly believe you are the same person you were a few years earlier because of your enlightened state of mind.

Students

If you are missing I and R in your name, you are here to learn all the qualities described at the beginning of this Chance. To be missing those letters from your entire name is rare but it does occur. This indicates you overlooked the human, feeling, emotional side of your life until this life. Emotional mastery is your challenge. Emotions in you could be up and down like a yo-yo until this Chance Number 9 is confronted, processed, and the information learned is applied in your daily living.

Challenge

Do be patient with yourself. There is no need to be hard on yourself. You won't learn any faster by being hard on yourself so accept this Chance as a challenge and enjoy the process of learning. You can do it. The awareness of the fact this is one of your Chances is more than half the journey toward reaching the goal of experiencing and learning from it.

Children

Children learning this Chance may feel very tender-hearted, sympathetic, and compassionate at a young age or they may feel upset, disappointed, and disillusioned by their perception of people around them. Energy may be used either way. Emotional ups and downs would be a normal situation for these children because that is part of the nature of this Chance.

Reassure your child we are all brothers and sisters and of the oneness that connects us all. Help children understand when they have expectations of others, they set themselves up for the perceived disappointment they feel if those expectations are not met. Help them learn to accept and love themselves and accept and love others.

Your child would notice if another child was being "picked on" on the playground at school. Unkind behavior would bother him or her and you might hear about the incident when you ask about your child's day. Allow emotion and feelings to be expressed in appropriate ways.

Teach children thought comes first and then the feeling. Children can control their emotions by what they think. Encourage them to give of themselves because they want to, they choose to. Encouraging children to focus on living present moments to the best of their ability helps them avoid noticing the perceived "flaws" in others.

Special Significance

If you have only one I or R in your entire name, this is a significant trait and deserves special discussion, which I hope will be very helpful to you.

Shoulds

You have a wonderful value system and a strong list of "shoulds" as to how you behave, cope, and live. You run into perceived difficulty because of your mistaken belief that everyone has the same system. When other people don't live up to your "shoulds" you feel disappointed, let down, possibly a lack of support, or devastated, depending on the intensity of your feelings.

People have a right to be who they are, to have their own list of "shoulds." The list may actually be similar to yours but their priorities may be slightly different. You may want others to change to make you feel more comfortable. You feel hurt, sad, angry, or a whole range of emotion when you want something from someone you believe you are not getting.

Irrational Thoughts

Wanting other people to change so you feel more comfortable is absolutely irrational. You set yourself up for the disappointment you feel when you have expectations about how someone will respond, react, or behave. You honestly set yourself up for that. People are just being themselves. Release people to be themselves, and learn to meet your own needs. Accept people as they are.

Your Focus

Remember every rose has a thorn. On which will you choose to focus? The rose or the thorns? When you are focusing on the rose you feel love, warmth, harmony, and joy. You are really focusing on the Christ Consciousness in everyone and everything.

You feel anger, bitterness, fear, anxiety, resentful, and judgmental when you choose to focus on the perceived thorns in people and situations. You have no control over someone else. So why focus on someone you upset yourself over but have no power to change?

Gullible

When you have only one of the letters, you may be somewhat gullible. You could be "taken" because you are inexperienced in human relationships and too trusting for your own good. "I have this bridge in Brooklyn I want to talk to you about buying...you'll love having your own bridge."

If you contract for anything that involves a major outlay of money, or time, no matter how honest the salesperson's face is hear yourself saying something like "That sounds wonderful, I want the agreement in writing." There is no need to feel self-conscious about saying that. You have every right to be businesslike in conducting your affairs and you save yourself a lot of stress. Does that make sense to you? I think the insight could be very helpful.

There is no need to think you are "bad" if you are perceived as gullible and easily "taken." I would rather be the one who trusts than the one who wants to capitalize on my trusting nature. The perceived con artist has lessons to learn, right? Your awareness of what you are learning will help you to be wiser, because when you know better you will do better.

Your Share of Responsibility

No one can "take advantage" of you unless you play a part in it. In the first place, the thought someone has "taken advantage" of you is your perception. Your thought is a judgment. You always play a part in whatever you choose to upset yourself over.

No one has the power to make you upset. You always create your upset by reacting instead of responding. Reacting is to feel like a victim and you give the other person lots of power over you when you react.

Responding is choosing what you will say or do because you know you, and only you, are responsible for what you think and how you feel as a result of what you thought. The thought always comes first to program your computer brain to produce the feeling in your body.

Speak Up

You feel anger and resentment toward someone when you do not speak up and say what you want. Many times other people have no idea you even want something from them.

Family members are notorious for believing "If you really loved me you would know what I want you to do." This belief is another totally irrational one that helps keep you feeling anxious, irritable, fearful, and unhappy. Do you enjoy maintaining the "poor me" image more than you enjoy taking responsibility for yourself and speaking up? You always have the choice. You aren't honest with yourself or the other person though when you choose not to discuss what you want from them.

Meet Your Needs Happily

Maybe your first irrational thought is someone else should do something for you to make you happy. Make yourself happy. If you want flowers, candy, or a special item you believe would not be forthcoming from another person, arrange a remembrance for yourself and feel good about the process. If you arrange something and feel like a martyr, the step taken was self-defeating.

If you live with a person who seems hesitant about asserting him or herself in business dealings, with bank tellers, store clerks, or people around them and you are willing to assert yourself, do it and feel good. Why would you assert yourself and then put the other person "down" because they didn't. You make yourself unhappy and a bit crazy by holding that viewpoint because it is irrational.

The perceived non-assertive person may be learning to accept (Chance Number 2). You may be learning to take charge and stand on your own two feet (Chance Number 1). Stop judging and labeling. Stop doing that. Whatever you are doing, do with love or don't do it.

Conclusion

The Equalizer

I told you the good news of you on all of these pages. You know there is no need to brag to anyone, or feel superior regarding your Chances because all the Chances are wonderful. The fact you may have all 9 Chances and beautifully balanced is no basis for boasting either, because you are obviously here for a reason. On the other hand there is no need to use the fact you may have several Chances missing as an excuse for inappropriate behavior. People who feel good about themselves do not need to brag or look for excuses. You know that now. The message is to accept and love.

Responsible Parenting

If you are a parent you have a responsibility and right to guide your child in a loving manner and to set rules and boundaries. I am convinced children feel more secure and loved when parents set appropriate limits and gradually allow more and more choices for the child as the youngster demonstrates ability to assume responsibility. Human children are not able to stand on their own as quickly as animal children. Parents are in a responsible position for a reason and need to assume that role until children are able to be responsible for themselves.

You are not always good to your children if you hand them material things when they are old enough to earn part or all of the money themselves. Making things "too easy" really deprives your child of the wonderful feeling which comes from setting a goal and working toward it to achieve a conclusion. There is no conflict whatsoever with what I have said about feeling good about yourself and your role as a parent. I want to be sure you understand that.

Your Cleansing

Well, bless your heart, did you get the message? Are you convinced to let go of blame, bitterness, and resentment because your experiences were all opportunities you attracted, for your own growth and development? Your best interest is served by releasing all unhappy perceptions. You know now if it wasn't your specific situations it would have been similar ones. You wanted to stretch yourself and learn in those areas.

Your Healing

Did you forgive whomever you feel you need to forgive? Did you also forgive yourself? Not because you did anything "wrong" (you always do the best you can), but forgive yourself for having wanted something so much from someone that you felt you didn't get. That's the point where healing occurs in your body.

Go For It

The only way you could possibly miss the clear, positive message in this book is if you are absolutely determined to punish and hate yourself always. I don't believe anyone fits that description.

There is no need to organize study groups to discuss this material. That would be a cop-out. You got the message. You know you did. Go out and live it.

Inspirational Reading

• *A Course in Miracles,* P.O.Box 635 Tiburon, CA 94920,
  Foundation for Inner Peace, 1980

• Bach, Richard, *Illusions,* New York: Dell Publishers, 1981.

• Carnegie, Dale E., *How to Win Friends and Influence People,*
  New York: Pocketbooks, 1990.

• Cousins, Norman, *Anatomy of an Illness,* New York:
  Bantam Publications, 1986.

• Dyer, Wayne, *Your Erroneous Zones,* New York:,
  HarperCollins, 1993.

• Dyer, Wayne, *Pulling Your Own Strings,* New York:
  HarperCollins, 1994.

• Maltz, Maxwell, *Psycho-Cybernetics,* New York: Pocketbooks, 1987

• Peale, Norman Vincent, *Power of Positive Thinking,* New York:
  Fawcett, 1987.

• Steadman, Alice, *Who's the Matter With Me,*
  Espress Publishers, 1985.

About the Author

9 Chances to Feel Good About Yourself is the result of repeated requests from thousands of individuals Judy Laslie counseled to feel better about themselves, their loved ones, associates, employees, and others. People look at life in a more positive, holistic way after hearing her views.

After graduating from Ball State University, Judy launched a teaching career which led to further education at workshops in Transactional Analysis, cognitive therapy, stress reduction, assertiveness, journal writing, holistic healing, metaphysics, parapsychology, and handwriting analysis. She studied universal truths with the International Order of Coptics, experienced Dr. Romero's Symposium, and was initiated into First Degree Reiki. Judy is also a graduate of Silva Mind Control and has been a member of Spiritual Frontiers Fellowship International for many years.

Her personal appearances include talk radio, special interest fairs, fundraisers, garden clubs, graduation all night parties, church guilds, luncheons, private gatherings, social events, and guest lecturing in classrooms.

An award winning health food store is her current base of operation as she counsels people on marriage, health, bereavement, wayward children, business, and careers. Individually created cassette tapes based on the information in *9 Chances to Feel Good About Yourself* are already in many states of the U.S. as well as in England, France, Germany, Ireland, Italy, and Japan. She is mother to three grown children, wife to her college sweetheart and probably would tell you she's still trying to figure out what she's going to be when she " grows-up." She is a seeker who also knows how to "bloom where she grows."

"A clear, concise formula for living life with purpose and enthusiasm. Serves as a wonderful road map for the mind and heart."
The Reverend Karen Boland

"...the general philosophy...works well. You have given so much to guide people. Your book serves a great need."
Gwen Frostic, Michigan Poet and Artist

This holistic book explains how to increase your awareness and let go of resentment, bitterness, regret, and old beliefs that keep you feeling unhappy, miserable, unloved, or victimized. **9 Chances to Feel Good About Yourself** offers sound universal truths gathered from many disciplines and presented in logical sequence to turn your life around now.

Learn to understand:

- how life really works
- where *problems* originate
- how to resolve *stumbling blocks*
- what lessons you want to learn
- how thoughts create
- how to *bloom where you grow*

Learn how to free yourself of stress by using positive self-talk and other proven techniques to feel love, warmth, and harmony within you and experience a healthy, joyous, dynamic, rewarding life. You have choices. Do you want to feel good? Good feelings about you then spread to others like the ever-increasing circles of influence surrounding a pebble thrown into a pond.

9 Chances to Feel Good About Yourself has a unique format in that readers are active participants in applying information received in Part I to determine specific, personal, predictable aspects of themselves described in Part II. Enjoy learning to accept and love yourself. You might even learn to love a rainy day.

Personal Tape Order Form

The author counsels in self-understanding on 60 minute personally individualized tapes based on expanded information in *9 Chances to Feel Good About Yourself.* Your name and your birth date are the outline of your life including the lessons you want to learn, what motivates you, how others see you, your talents, and internal dynamics. The information is a positive umbilical cord from you to you that is valid always. It never needs updating.

This is a much appreciated gift for parents of a new baby, a birthday, anniversary, bar/bat mitzvah, special holiday like Father's Day, graduation, anyone wanting to make a big decision, or anyone wanting to see his or her life in a more positive way.

_____

print full exact birth name clearly
(be sure spelling is correct, include Jr. or II if applicable)

Birth date_____/_____/_____
　　　　　　　month　　day　　year
(time of birth is not required)

Accurate information is only available with complete, exact name at birth. Do not use a confirmation name. Clerical errors on birth certificate are not valid, use name intended. The author assumes no responsibility for redoing a tape due to inaccurate information given initially.

To: *Judy Laslie*
2371 Radnor, Birmingham, MI 48009

Please send _____copies $90. each U.S. funds
(No charge for shipping & handling or sales tax)
Enclosed is my check payable to *Judy Laslie* for $_____

from_____

address_____

city_____state_____zip_____

Please allow 4 weeks for delivery.
Indicate name and address for gifts sent directly.

Thank you for your order.

Book Order Form

9chances.com

A feast of simply stated universal truths for living fully and joyously. Logical, loving, and easy to apply, *9 Chances to Feel Good About Yourself* is a refreshing outlook on life. Reviewed by psychologists, motivators, religious and spiritual leaders, the new 128-page paperback has a title which truly lives up to its promise and is available for you now.

To: **Judy Laslie**
      2371 Radnor
      Birmingham, MI 48009

Please send ___copies $14.95 each U.S. funds.
      (No charge for shipping & handling or sales tax)

Enclosed is my check payable to Judy Laslie for
$_____

from_____

address_____

city_____state_____zip_____

Indicate name and address for gifts sent directly.

Thank you for your order.

chances@9chances.com